PIERS PLOWMAN: THE A-TEXT

An Alliterative Verse Translation

pegasus paperbooks

Piers Plowman: The A-Text

An Alliterative Verse Translation

FRANCIS DOLORES COVELLA, S.C.

Wm. Langland

Introduction and Notes

DAVID C. FOWLER

Medieval & Renaissance Texts & Studies
Binghamton, New York
1992

Library of Congress Cataloging-in-Publication Data

Langland, William, 1130?–1400?
[Piers the Plowman]
Piers Plowman: the A-text: an alliterative verse translation / by Francis Dolores Covella; introduction and notes by David C. Fowler.
p. cm. – (PEGASUS PAPERBOOKS)
ISBN 0-86698-120-9 (pbk.)
1. Christian poetry, English (Middle)—Modernized versions. I. Covella, Francis Dolores. II. Fowler, David C., 1921– . III. Title
PR2013.C67 1992
821′.1—dc20 92-16912
CIP

Printed in the United States of America

To the Undergraduates
of the College of Mount Saint Vincent
Riverdale, New York

Contents

Introduction

The earliest version of the English alliterative poem *Piers Plowman* (called the "A" text) can be dated 1362, a time when the glories of the reign of Edward III in England were past; the nation was losing its grip on France, and was experiencing civil unrest at home. Suddenly an unknown poet spoke to the people in a powerful prophetic voice, calling for the establishment of justice in the gate. Less than twenty years later, in June of 1381, came the uprising known as the Peasants' Revolt, which drew its ideology and passion from this poem, and came uncomfortably close to effecting a cultural revolution of the working class. But the prospect of such a sudden overthrow of the established order produced an overwhelming reaction, resulting in the crushing of the revolt and its leadership. In like manner the revolutionary message of the original version of *Piers Plowman* was soon stifled in two revisions (called the B and C texts) made during the 1380s that spiritualized the plowman and altered the message of the poem. Since the fourteenth century the attention of readers and critics has been mainly devoted to these revised forms, while the original A text of 1362 has been largely ignored. Hence it is important to emphasize that this volume offers, for the first time, a modern translation of the complete A version, recognized as a poem in its own right. The following remarks are designed to introduce *Piers Plowman* in its original form, as it was read in the 1360s and 1370s, when no other form of the poem existed.

England in Mid-Century (1346–1362)

The notorious reign of Edward II (1307–1327) ended dramatically in September 1327 with the king's deposition and subsequent murder in Berkeley Castle. Under the circumstances, things did not look promising for his son Edward III (1327–1377). But the young king, who was as different from his father as could be imagined, quickly took over leadership of the nation and marshaled his forces for a war with France, which began in 1337 and led to a spectacular victory at Crecy in 1346. Other military triumphs followed, over both Scotland and France, and the successful outcome of the siege of Calais in 1347 enabled the English fleet to dominate the Channel, and from this seaport launch their attacks directly against France. The highlight of Edward's continental campaigns, now increasingly under the leadership of his son Edward (the Black Prince), was undoubtedly the capture of the French King John at Poitiers in 1356. Thereafter the English began to suffer reverses, along with a certain amount of fatigue, reaching its nadir on Black Monday (14 April 1360), when the king and his forces outside Paris were overawed by a dark cloud, which brought with it a freak hailstorm and bitter weather resulting in numerous deaths by freezing. The following month, Edward III signed a treaty at Bretigny near Chartres waiving his claim to the French throne. But the English king did not come away entirely empty-handed: in addition to retaining Calais and certain territories, he obtained the promise of 3,000,000 crowns from the dauphin as ransom for the return of his father King John.

Through much of the fourteenth century, the papacy was established in costly exile in Avignon, far removed from Rome and the customary sources of its income. Moreover the Avignon popes tended to side with France in the conflict with England, so that their efforts to bring about peace had little effect. Even before the Great Schism (1378–1417), which began with an exchange of anathemas between Urban VI in Rome and Clement VII in Avignon, it was evident that the control of the papacy over both church and state in western Europe was rapidly slipping away. So much for the great dream of Innocent III.

As papal power declined, ecclesiastical appointments to high position in the English church came increasingly under the control of the English crown. Church historian W. A. Pantin has pointed out a striking feature in the evolution of episcopal appointments in the thirteenth and fourteenth centuries: in the earlier period the reform bishops were distinguished scholars, while in the fourteenth century the bishops increasingly tended to be strong administrators and astute politicians rather than learned men. This important change made itself felt throughout the ecclesiastical establishment, all the way down to the parish level, and is even reflected in the satirical portraits of worldly churchmen in the prologue to Chaucer's *Canterbury Tales*. Especially in the latter half of the century, it was evident that the Christian Church in England was rapidly becoming a temple of the kingdom (Amos 7:15).

Despite its growing worldliness, the Church itself still produced articulate critics of the established order. Some of this criticism appeared in the (largely anonymous) literature of social satire, but, as G. R. Owst has shown, much of it was uttered fearlessly from the pulpit by legions of conscientious preachers. An impartial observer in the fourteenth century would have seen in the English church a house divided against itself: on the one hand, there were the "regular" clergy, living on vast and wealthy estates, acquisitive, socially conservative, and bent on preserving the status quo; on the other hand, there were the "secular" clergy, from whose ranks came the priests who served their parishes in the manner of Chaucer's humble parson. Neither of these groups had a monopoly on righteousness, but it was clearly from the secular clergy that a challenge to the social order would have to come. Between these two groups stood the friars, and the stresses that produced the cleavage between seculars and regulars also brought about a division within the fraternal orders, particularly the Franciscans, whose members disagreed on the question of apostolic poverty. The Conventuals took a more conservative line, while the Spiritual Franciscans insisted that Christ and the Apostles had not owned property, and that this was intended as a model for the Christian life. Clearly their position was not designed to make the "possessioners" feel comfortable, and in 1323 a bull issued by Pope John XXII declared this a heretical interpretation.

By mid-century it was clear that the Spiritual Franciscans had lost control of the fraternal movement. The orders retained a kind of fictional poverty, largely by assigning custody of their houses and property to laymen while retaining actual possession. According to the rule, they were not to touch money; they got around this by wearing gloves. Still, this is only one side of the picture. The friars had produced a succession of great scholars during the early days of reform, mainly the thirteenth century; even in the period we are studying they retain a strong emphasis on education, at least enough to arouse jealousy in the secular clergy, whose ranks were not without their share of ignorant priests. The hostility between these groups was particularly evident in Oxford, and the former chancellor of the university, Richard FitzRalph, delivered sermons critical of the friars in London from the pulpit of Saint Paul's in 1356/57, and these were matched with sermons by fraternal preachers highly critical of the secular clergy. To the pious London worshiper it must have seemed that Manasseh was devouring Ephraim, and Ephraim Manasseh. But behind all these conflicts and passionate arguments lay a genuine concern for the proper role of the Church in dealing with the escalating problems of wealth, poverty, war, and corruption as they affected both church and state.

In the midst of war, schism, oppression, and greed, were there any signs of God's displeasure? Indeed there were. Across the face of Europe and to the shores of England in 1348–49 came the pestilence known as the Black Death. An entire population stood helpless in the path of the king of terrors. A general power was given to all priests, both secular and regular, to hear confession and grant absolution, while the mortality rate for the clergy itself was awesome. Prices at first slumped, because no one sought to buy anything out of a general fear of death; and the ordinary functions of society broke down, since, according to Knighton, "there was such a great scarcity of servants that no one knew what he ought to do" (Dobson, 60). The scholarly Thomas Bradwardine, newly consecrated archbishop of Canterbury, arrived in London in August 1349 and was dead within two days. Countless generations had been told repeatedly that the social order to which they belonged had been established by God. Now for the first time it may have become possible for many to question the permanence of that order, and to think that there might be alternatives to it. The plague changed everything; there is scarcely a single development in the remainder of the century that does not owe something to its impact. It is no coincidence that in a few short years there emerged the popular rhyme:

> When Adam delved and Eve span,
> Who was then the gentleman?

Whatever might have been in the hearts and minds of the people, it was the king and council who first responded to the catastrophe, and this response took the form of a statute designed to force laborers to remain on the job and to freeze wages at pre-plague levels. The initial action of 1349 was followed in 1351 by the more severe Statute of Laborers, which was designed to hold the workers in check. Needless to say the law was not well received; in a severely reduced population, laborers were very much in demand, and the natural tendency was for wages to rise, as indeed they did, despite repeated legislation by a succession of parliaments.

When ancient Israel suffered a catastrophic earthquake, Isaiah quoted their reaction as: "The bricks have fallen down, but we will build them with hewn stones," a far cry from the response demanded by the prophet: "For the people turneth not unto him that smiteth them, neither do they seek the Lord of hosts" (Isa. 9:10, 13). In like manner, rather than seeking the Lord, the English leadership turned to mechanisms for preserving the status quo in the face of disaster . This absence of moral seriousness, in fact, seems to have characterized English government policy for the remainder of the reign of the aging Edward III. Neither the vicious return of the pestilence in 1361 nor the growing resentment of an oppressed people seems to have affected the policies of either church or state. But at this very moment, a prophet arose whose message is preserved for us in the earliest version of the poem known as *Piers Plowman*. And it was this version—*not* the revisions that appeared later—which was to be embraced and exploited by the leaders of the Peasants' Revolt.

Piers Plowman: The A Version (1362)

A glance at the poem as a whole shows us that it is in reality two poems; the first, called the *Visio* (Vision), contains an introductory section (a prologue and passus I or book I); an allegorical action set in London at Westminster (passus II–IV); a pivotal confession of the cardinal sins (passus V); a second allegorical action in a rural setting introducing Piers, the good plowman (passus VI–VII); and, finally, a dramatic conclusion in which Piers is given a pardon by St. Truth, and the Dreamer awakens (passus VIII). This *Visio* is followed immediately by a second and related poem entitled "The Life of Dowel Dobetter and Dobest," consisting of a prologue, passus I, and passus II (A passus IX–XI), usually referred to as the *Vita* (Life), after the first word of its Latin title. Although the *Vita* is also in the form of a dream, there is no real allegorical action. Instead, various allegorical spokesmen seek to answer the Dreamer's questions concerning what consitutes a truly upright life and where in the various ranks of society it may be found.

In the opening of the *Visio*, the poet tells us that on a May morning in Malvern hills he paused beside a stream, weary with wandering, and soon went to sleep to the sound of its waters (A Prol. 11–19):

> Then did I dream a marvelous dream,
> That I was in a wilderness; I did not know where.
> And as I looked toward the east in the light of the sun,
> I saw a tower on a hill artfully made.
> Beneath was a deep dale a dungeon within
> With a ditch deep and dark and dreadful to see.
> A fair field full of folk I found there between
> Of all kinds of people, the poor and the rich,
> Working and wandering as the world requires.

In this prologue the poet shows us the everyday world of fourteenth-century England against a backdrop of eternity: heaven and hell, as represented by the tower and the dungeon. Thus the standard Christian values are to be used to judge the behavior of the folk in the field. It is quickly apparent that some are good and others bad. Some plow the land and work hard, while "wasters" greedily consume what the workers produce. Worthy anchorites stay in their cells, unlike those who wander about the countryside living a life of self-indulgence. There are good minstrels, a legitimate profession, but there are also "tale-tellers and jesters, Judas' children," who play the fool even though they have the intelligence to work for a living if they would. There are beggars who feign handicaps for food, fight in the alehouses, and lead lives of ribaldry and sloth.

In his roll call of the professions, the Dreamer presents a series of vignettes reminiscent of Chaucer's portraits in the General Prologue of

The Canterbury Tales. Indeed a storytelling pilgrimage like that of Chaucer is briefly described (A Prol. 46–49):

> Pilgrims and palmers promised each other
> To seek the shrine of Saint James and saints at Rome;
> They went forth on their way with many wise tales,
> And had leave to lie all their lives after.

At the end of their journey, instead of the customary indulgence, these pilgrims are granted permission to tell lies for the rest of their lives: the poet's contempt for such pilgrimages is quite evident, both here and later on in the poem.

In the field we see friars preaching to the people for personal profit, glossing the gospel to make it conform to their greed. These friars, unlike their predecessors, are well-dressed, and make it their business to hear the confessions of great lords, not the common people. And the Dreamer adds ominously: unless Holy Church and these friars can hold together, the greatest mischief on earth is rapidly approaching. In these lines the poet seems to allude to the hostilities between friars and seculars made public in the sermons at Saint Paul's (1356–57).

There is little love for pardoners in fourteenth-century satirical literature: even Chaucer seems to regard his pardoner as the one unredeemable soul in the company on the road to Canterbury. Equally reprehensible is the one who appears among the folk of the field (A Prol. 65–72):

> A pardoner preached there as if he were priest;
> Presented a scroll with seals of the bishop
> And said he himself could absolve them all there
> Of feigning to fast and of holy vows broken.
> The unlearned liked him and believed what he said,
> Came up on their knees and kissed the decree.
> He poked at them with his brevet and bleared their eyes,
> And raked in with this ragman rings and brooches.

There is anger in this description, but it is also controlled, with a skillful play on words. The pardoner pokes the people in the face with his scroll, "blearing their eyes" (which also means to deceive), and then uses the scroll like a croupier's stick to rake in the offerings. But our poet cannot long sustain this ironical detachment, and so he angrily addresses the poor victims of the pardoner's guile: Thus you give your gold to help gluttons, and leave it with lechers! If the bishop who allowed his seal to be used were truly blessed, the people might not be deceived; and the guilt must be shared by those parish priests who allow the pardoner to preach and then divide the offering with him. All of them are taking money that should go to the poor people of the parish.

Are the secular clergy any better than the others? Parsons and parish priests complain that the pestilence has reduced their income, and ask their bishop for permission to go to London "to sing there for simony, for silver is sweet." And what about lawyers (A Prol. 84–89)?

> There hovered a hundred in hoods of pure silk,
> Sergeants, it seemed, who served at the bar,
> Pleaded for profit and expounded the law;
> Not for love of our Lord would they open their lips.
> You might better mete the mist on Malvern's high hills,
> Than get a mumble from their mouth until money was showed.

The roll call continues with ecclesiastics of all ranks, from bishop to deacon, going to London to take lucrative positions in the government as accountants or clerks of the king's bench. All ranks of society are represented in the field, from barons to bondmen, and many crafts: bakers, butchers, brewers, weavers, tailors, masons, miners, ditchers, and delvers. The prologue ends with the refrain of a popular song mingling with London street cries.

The prologue of *Piers Plowman* has taught us to expect a balanced treatment of the various representatives of society. But we are not to demand impartiality, for, subtly but surely, the sheep are to be separated from the goats: those whose allegiance is to the tower are distinguished from those destined for the dungeon. Already we have seen hints that members of the establishment in London, both church and state, are corrupt, and that integrity is to be found, if anywhere, in the hinterlands among those who put themselves to the plow. In the words of Micah (1:5): "What is the transgression of Jacob? Is it not Samaria?"

From the tower on the hill comes a lovely lady to answer the Dreamer's questions and expound the basic Christian doctrines that are to guide his understanding throughout the poem, both *Visio* and *Vita*. In function she is reminiscent of Boethius's Lady Philosophy, but in fact she is Holy Church, and she begins by reviewing for the Dreamer certain fundamentals of Christian teaching. In the tower, she says, is Truth (God), who created you to worship him during your life on earth. He has given you clothing, food, and drink for your nourishment, and it is up to you not to use anything (such as drink) to excess (A I 33–35):

> Measure is medicine, though you yearn for more.
> All is not good for the spirit what the senses demand,
> Nor support for the body what pleases the soul.

With such trenchant wisdom Holy Church warns the Dreamer against the dangers of the world, the flesh, and the devil. Believe not your body, she adds—in case her listener was foolish enough to think that the gut is always right—for a liar teaches your flesh in order to betray you if he can.

To whom does the money of this world belong? asks the Dreamer, and the lady replies (Mark 12:17): "Render to Caesar the things that are

Caesar's, and to God the things that are God's." Entrust your worldly treasure to reason and common sense. She then goes on to tell him that Wrong inhabits the dungeon in the dale, the "father of falsehood," that is the devil, who incited Adam and Eve to disobedience, counseled Cain to kill his brother, and deceived Judas with Jewish silver.

When the Dreamer wonderingly asks who she is, the lady responds with "Holy Church am I—you ought to know me: I received you first (at the baptismal font), and taught you your faith." Whereupon the Dreamer falls to his knees and asks her to tell him how to save his soul. "Truth is the best," says the lady, taking as her text "Deus caritas" (God is love, 1 John 4:8). "For he who lives by truth, trustworthy in his speech, his deeds matching his words, with malice toward none, is called a god by the gospel" (Luke 6:35; cf. Ps. 82:6 and John 10:34).

The reader acquainted with doctrinal literature of the period will have noticed that the teaching of Holy Church is remarkable for its simplicity. The stance of the poet is that of the prophets (Amos 5:15): "Hate the evil, and love the good, and establish judgment in the gate." Do you want to avoid an eternity in the dungeon of Wrong? Then you must obey the teaching of the Bible (A I 119–22):

> But they who work by the word that Holy Writ teaches,
> And end, as I've said, in perfect works,
> May be sure that their souls shall ascend into heaven
> Where Truth is in Trinity and receives them in triumph.

In short, "Be ye therefore perfect" (Matt. 5:48). And the lady concludes her sermon with a curious exhortation (A I 125–26):

> Teach this to laymen, for the learned know it,
> That Truth is the choicest treasure on earth.

If we have not yet perceived the poet's viewpoint, we might jump to the conclusion that all is well with learned men, who know the gospel, and that it is the poor who stand in desperate need. But as we shall see, it is in fact the plowmen of this world who are destined for salvation, while the educated class, in both church and state, are sinking down into hell. This point is brought out in the conclusion to passus I by one of the author's favorite devices: he has the Dreamer ask a foolish question which triggers an angry response from his teacher (A I 127–32):

> "I have no innate knowledge," said I, "so you must teach me
> Where in my body this knowledge begins."
> "You dumb dolt," said she, "your wits are quite dull.
> Inborn understanding instructs you in the heart
> To love your Lord better than you love yourself
> And to avoid deadly sin though you should die."

The Dreamer here plays the role of the intellectual, intent on an understanding of psychological process, rather than simple acceptance of the divine imperative. After her initial angry explosion, Lady Holy Church patiently and movingly describes how the love of God was expressed by Christ's death on the cross. This love, she continues, was meant to be an example to us: the rich should help the poor, and priests should set an example of generosity to their parishioners (A I 146–73). These lines should be read aloud, with feeling, so that their tone can be appreciated. The poet is evenhanded in his criticism of all ranks, including laborers, but some feel the heat of his passion more than others. This is an angry passage, in which rich people and avaricious chaplains are rebuked by a poet who is alienated from them, and has little hope that they will respond to his criticisms. "And I will smite the winter house with the summer house; and the houses of ivory shall perish, and the great houses shall have an end, saith the Lord" (Amos 3:15). Holy Church is more careful than Amos to remind the listener of God's positive mandate (A I 178–79):

> Love is the dearest thing our Lord asks of us,
> And also the highway that leads into heaven.

But her message to the rich and powerful is just as severe.

Lady Meed at Westminster

Before Holy Church bids farewell to the Dreamer, she draws back a curtain (as it were) in one part of the field, to reveal a gathering of people around Lady Meed, who is to hold center stage in the first allegorical action. "Meed" means reward, or, as it turns out, bribery, and so it is not surprising that around this lady are gathered the various officers and practitioners who make up the government of the nation. These corrupt functionaries seek to bring about a marriage between Meed and Falsehood, and they end up at the seat of the English government in Westminster, where the king is advised by Conscience and Reason to prohibit the marriage (A II–IV). After the cleansing of society in the confession scene (A V), the people turn to Piers, the humble plowman, to lead them to Truth (A VI–VIII). Thus we see that the *Visio* as a whole is dominated by the two figures of Lady Meed and Piers, representatives on earth of the dungeon and the tower. We are clearly told which side we should choose, but the genius of the author shows in his ability to reveal the complexity of the social problems he addresses, even as he simultaneously deflates the pretensions of the worldly through irony and satire.

In obedience to Holy Church's command, the Dreamer looks to his left (A II 7–4):

> I looked on the left side as the lady instructed,

And was aware of a woman wonderfully clothed,
Her robe edged with fur, the richest on earth,
Crowned with a crown, the king has none better.
All her five fingers were fretted with rings
Of the most precious stones that prince ever wore.
Robed in red scarlet and ribboned with gold,
There lives no lady more lovely than she.

Who is this woman? asks the Dreamer, and in her parting speech Holy Church leaves us in no doubt. She has often annoyed me, the lady says, and criticized my teaching to lords. In the pope's palace she is as familiar as I am, but she should not be so, for Wrong is her sire, while I come of a higher lineage (God). She then informs the Dreamer of the intended marriage of Meed and False. Stay away from all these if you wish to dwell with Truth! She then commends him to the Lord, and leaves him to interpret what he sees with no further help from her. Nevertheless, as we shall see, the Dreamer will not be without assistance from particular spokesmen for Truth such as Theology, Conscience, and Reason, all of whom speak out at critical moments in the drama.

The first to protest is Theology, when he hears the feoffment (in the form of a pact with the devil) prepared by False for his marriage with Meed, and proclaimed publicly by Simony and Civil Law. In protesting this marriage Theology claims that Meed is actually a legitimate offspring of Amends (payment for services rendered), and that God intends to give Meed to Truth: "for the workman is worthy of his meat" (Matt. 10:10). After denouncing Simony and Civil for ruining Holy Church and harming the people, Theology tells them to take Meed to London and get a legal opinion on the proposed marriage.

The intervention of Theology triggers a grimly amusing scene in which all the machinery of bribery is set in motion to arrange the legalization of Meed's marriage to False in the court at Westminster. Favel (Flattery) fetches florins, ordering Guile to distribute them to Simony, Civil, and Falsewitness, who in turn promise False that they will make Meed his lawfully wedded wife. Amid all this hubbub there is a cry for horses, and Favel quickly fetches forth beasts of burden: Meed sits on a sheriff, False on a juryman, Simony and Civil on a pair of summoners, while bishops ride on deans and subdeans decked out like warhorses. A commissioner (bishop's deputy) is hitched to Civil's cart and ordered to fetch supplies from fornicators, while Liar pulls a large wagon carrying the remaining crowd of fools and deceivers. Behind this artful allegory we may detect not only a sense of humor but also moral outrage. The commissioner's use of a system of fines as a source of personal income is especially repugnant, and reminds us of Amos's angry denunciation of fines used by the Israelite priesthood to maintain the Temple wine supply (Amos 2:8).

Word of this legal conspiracy reaches the king, who orders the arrest of the ringleaders, and specifically commands that Meed be brought before him. But Dread hears the king's instructions and hurries to warn the conspirators. Terrified, Falseness flies to the friars, Guile escapes and is hired as a merchant's apprentice, while Liar lurks through lanes, unwelcome and driven off because of his many tales. We then follow the trail of this fugitive as he is taken in by pardoners, physicians, grocers, messengers, and friars. He helps the pardoners turn indulgences into merchandise; he is invited to conduct urinalyses for physicians; he shows grocers how to use additives to sell their decaying food; he hangs out with minstrels and messengers; and he is dressed as a friar and invited to stay with them as often as he wishes. When all the conspirators have fled, only Lady Meed remains; and she trembles and weeps when she is arrested.

Despite the fact that Meed is technically in custody when she arrives in London, she is warmly received, for, as the poet remarks, "those residing at Westminster all worship her there" (A III 12). A delegation of justices calls on the lady and promises to help her gain the approval of the king, in spite of all that Conscience may do. Meed rewards them richly, and promises quick advancement to a group of clerks who offer to help her. A friar volunteers to be her confessor, assuring her that for a small consideration he will forgive her any and all sins, and that if she should finance the glazing of one of their windows, not only would her name be inscribed in the glass for all to see, but her soul would be assured of salvation. At this point the poet's restraint deserts him, and he speaks out angrily against such abuses. God strictly prohibited engraving of names when he said "Let not thy left hand know what thy right hand doeth" (Matt. 6:3). Those who thus proclaim their good deeds in public should beware lest worldly recognition be their only recompense, as our Savior said: "Verily I say unto you, they have their reward" (Matt. 6:2).

One other abuse that triggers the poet's wrath is Meed's attempt to bribe the mayor of London. She intercedes on behalf of retailers, who are offering bribes so that the mayor, as the one charged with enforcement, will not crack down when they inflate their prices. "For my love," says that lady, "love them each one, and suffer them to sell somewhat unreasonably" (A III 79–80). But as the author angrily points out, mayors and magistrates are appointed precisely to punish those who prey on poor people who must buy piecemeal. Instead they get rich through such bribes, with what the poor should be putting in their stomachs. You can be sure that if these officials were not corrupt, they would not build themselves such magnificent homes, nor would they own so many tenements. They had better remember what Scripture says about this (Job 15:34): "fire shall consume the tabernacles of bribery." Although the poet is "merely" quoting the Bible here, the passage might well have caused corrupt officials to tremble. In less than twenty years, some of the great houses of London were destined to go up in flames.

The remainder of passus III is taken up with a debate before the king between Meed and Conscience. The king wants to forgive the lady and give her in marriage to Conscience, but the latter will not agree and launches into a denunciation of Meed: she is unreliable and a source of corruption; she killed your father (Edward II), poisoned popes (perhaps Benedict XI?), and has damaged Holy Church; she allows herself to be kept by all who can pay for her, and she frustrates the judicial process; like Chaucer's summoner she knows that "purse is the archdeacon's hell," and pays off the bishop's commissioner without fear of bell, book, or candle; she is a good friend of pope, bishop, and parson; the king's justices are ruined by her, and a faithful man can make no headway in court against the blizzard of her florins; lawyers defend only the wealthy, and poor men have no power to bring suit against injustice, so powerful is Meed!

The king is impressed by Conscience's indictment, but allows the lady to defend herself, and it is a tribute to the poet's artistry that she does so very skilfully. You know very well, Conscience, she says, that you yourself have depended on me many times. I did not kill any king, as you falsely accused me of doing, whereas you courted military disaster by making the king interpret the dark cloud and the cold weather in France as God's disapproval of the war, whereas I encouraged him to adhere to his military objectives. If it had not been for you, and if I'd had my way, the king would have become lord of all France, the richest of all realms! Besides, kings, emperors, and even popes must have meed to provide sustenance for those that serve them; all ranks of society, from priest to beggar, require meed as recompense for their services. In short, meed makes the world go round.

To this persuasive presentation the king responds enthusiastically: "By Christ, it seems clear, Meed might be worthy the mastery to have!" (A III 213–14). But Conscience responds by distinguishing between "meed without measure," an unearned reward, and "a reasonable wage," just payment for services rendered. "Meed without measure" can be good, as when God graciously grants his servants on earth a heavenly reward, and it is bad when magistrates accept payment from evildoers; while "a reasonable wage" is as legitimate as barter, in which no money changes hands. In short, money is not in itself evil: everything depends on the use to which it is put. Once again the Bible is invoked: the good man is "He that putteth not out his money to usury, nor taketh reward against the innocent" (Ps. 15:5); it is corrupt officialdom "in whose hands is mischief, and their right hand is full of bribes" (Ps. 26:10).

Conscience concludes with a sermon based on 1 Samuel 15, which recounts the war between Israel and Amalek during the reign of Saul. The point of this story is that soldiers engaged in a holy war are not to take booty for themselves. Saul violated this rule when he allowed his troops to seize cattle and himself spared King Agag, perhaps with a view to collecting ransom. So it was meed that got the king in trouble: indeed God said to Samuel that Saul should die, and his hatred of this sin even extended to the king's descendants. I will not take the time, says Conscience, to point the moral (*culorum*) of this story: lest I get into trouble, I'll bring it to an end.

Whether the powers that be ever heard or read this sermon of Conscience is a matter of conjecture, but it seems altogether likely that some of the peasants did. Knighton reports that when the rebels were destroying John of Gaunt's palace, the Savoy, in June 1381 (Dobson, 184): "One of the criminals chose a fine piece of silver and hid it in his lap; when his fellows saw him carrying it, they threw him, together with his prize, into the fire, saying that they were lovers of truth and justice, not robbers and thieves." This incident is reminiscent of an earlier episode in the Bible involving holy war, when Achan son of Carmi was burned to death by Joshua for looting during the invasion of Canaan (Josh. 7). In any case it is noteworthy that the rebels sought to keep their forces under the discipline of holy war, thus showing that they understood very well the *culorum* of Conscience's sermon.

But we should be careful to distinguish between the future impact of the poem on others and the intention of the author at the time of writing. For an understanding of this we have only Conscience's dark prophecy (A III 257–62):

> I, Conscience, know this, for common sense taught me
> That reason shall reign and govern many realms.
> What happened to Agag shall happen to others;
> Samuel shall slay him and Saul shall be blamed,
> David be crowned and conquer them all,
> And one Christian King shall care for each one.

We are still fifteen years away from the death of Edward III: does the poet envision some kind of disruption during the inevitable transfer of power? If so, he sees it as a hopeful event, leading to the establishment of a king who will walk in the ways of David. Like the prophets of old, the author of the A text is fundamentally optimistic, despite his dire warnings about the state of the nation. Thus he allows Conscience to end his sermon, not with gloom and doom, but with faith in the future of the country. No more shall Meed be master, but instead love, lowness, and loyalty. If anyone goes against the truth, he shall receive strict justice, or even lose his life. No longer shall lawyers become wealthy, as they are now: they have become lordly, while real justice is poor and banished from society. Indeed, things are going to change (A III 272–73):

> But common sense shall come yet, together with conscience,

> And make of law a laborer, such love shall arise.

Having heard both sides, the king now insists on a reconciliation, and orders Conscience to kiss Lady Meed. But Conscience refuses to do anything without the advice of Reason, who is then sent for and set on the bench in Westminster between the king and his son (the Black Prince). Is it possible to implement Conscience's brave new world, where reason governs? In passus IV we are given a test case, in which the integrity of the king is pitted against corruption, and integrity wins.

Peace comes into parliament and registers a complaint against Wrong. It is quickly evident that Peace is an ordinary citizen, and Wrong is an unscrupulous and powerful lord. Wrong has raped and stolen and cheated with impunity, and even maintains a small army of retainers whose presence intimidates Peace and his neighbors and, until now, makes them reluctant to go to law. The poet confides that the king knew these charges were true, "for Conscience had told him" (A IV 48), suggesting that this king can see beyond the surface of things, will judge the poor with righteousness, and will "reprove with equity for the meek of the earth" (Isa. 11:4).

Indeed the king's integrity is soon tested by a pair of shysters named Warren Wisdom and Witty, who advise Wrong to seek the help of Lady Meed. But when they approach the king with their bribes, the king orders Wrong to be put in irons, swearing, "Seven years shall he never see his feet once!" (A IV 73). Seeing that the king cannot be bought off, the two lawyers bring Meed to Peace and offer him compensation to settle out of court. Peace (the poor man) agrees with this, and appeals to the king to dismiss the charges against Wrong, but the latter refuses, declaring that such an action would encourage Wrong to break the law in the future. Unless Reason has pity on him, says the king, he shall remain in the stocks.

When the king's rigorous decision is announced, some beseech Reason to allow Meed to provide bail for the prisoner. Whereupon Reason launches into an eloquent statement of the conditions under which he is willing to have mercy on law breakers (A IV 100–110):

> "Counsel me not," said Reason, "to have compassion at all
> Until lords and ladies all love the truth,
> And Peronelle's fur be put in her closet,
> Till cherishing children be chastising with rods,
> Till the tales of entertainers be treated with scorn,
> Till clerks and knights speak with more courtesy,
> And repent of their ribaldry and repeat it no longer;
> Till priests ponder their preaching and apply it to themselves,
> And by their example inspire us to good;
> Till Saint James be sought where I shall assign,
> And no man go to Galicia unless he go forever. . . ."

From this it is clear that when Reason is finally willing to show mercy, mercy will no longer be necessary. As we shall see, this kind of militant irony is a recurrent feature of the A text, and will reappear later in Truth's pardon for Piers.

For the present, Reason summarizes his doctrine in the proverb, "No evil unpunished, no good unrewarded." If you follow this rule, he says, I will guarantee (A IV 130–31):

> That Law shall be laborer and lead afield dung,
> And Love shall lead your land as you surely would like.

When the court hears this verdict, Meed is laughed to scorn, Wisdom and Witty are for once left speechless, and the king asks Reason to stay with him as long as he lives. In the afterglow of this upbeat ending, we sense only a minor hint of hostility in the assignment of lawyers to the task of spreading manure in the fields. Twenty years later, however, the rebels marching on London were to kill every lawyer they encountered, just as a matter of principle. To what extent can "the power of the word" be invoked to link the poet's attitude toward lawyers with the deeds of the peasants? I do not favor any such connection, although for the author's own sake I trust that, by the time of the rising, death had "dealt him a dint."[1]

The Confession Scene

Next, the Dreamer sees the folk of the field assembled to hear a sermon by Conscience designed to prepare them for confession. In view of what we have noted earlier about the impact of the plague in 1361–1362, it is not surprising that Conscience uses this catastrophe to urge the people to turn unto him that smiteth them. He shows them that the pestilence resulted from sin, and that most recently it was pride that caused the great southwest wind on Saturday evening (15 January 1362): fruit trees were blown down, sinners, to warn you to do better! Beeches and oaks were flattened, turning tail upward as if in fear of the destruction that is certain to come before Doomsday.

But this is not a sermon on the Apocalypse. Conscience calls attention to these warning signs because he wants to see justice roll down like waters, and righteousness as a mighty stream (Amos 5:24). Like all true prophets, he is not merely "against sin"; he spells out exactly what the people are to do. Wasters are to go to work and earn a living by some craft; Purnel is to put away her finery; Thomas is to take two sticks and teach his wife how to stay out of trouble; Wat is to restrain his wife's

---

[1] See p. 105, n. 1.

appetite for expensive headdress; merchants are to discipline their children and not indulge them simply because they can afford it. He urges prelate and priest to obey their own sermons and set an example for the people. And what about the religious, who live under a monastic rule? Hold strictly to your rule, says Conscience, lest the king and his council put a crimp in your income, and take custody of it until you reform. And all you pilgrims who seek Saint James and saints of Rome: seek instead Saint Truth, for he may save you all.

In response to this eloquent appeal, representative sinners step forth from the crowd to confess. The general purpose of this scene is to depict the cleansing of society in preparation for the pilgrimage to Saint Truth recommended by Conscience. But like so many of the devices used in the poem, this episode provides incidental satire on human weaknesses represented by the personified sins. In this connection it is interesting to observe that these sins are not given equal time: Purnel, representing Pride, vows to remove her fine clothing and substitute a hair shirt in order to humble her high heart; Lechery merely swears to eat only one meal on Saturdays and go on the wagon ("drink with the duck"); Wrath does not appear at all in the A version, and one is tempted to conclude (barring accidental loss in copying) that the poet prefers not to denounce this sin, which might so easily be confused with righteous anger, an emotion that he clearly approves and has utilized in the writing of his poem. This leaves four sins that get most of the attention: Envy, Covetousness, Gluttony, and Sloth.

Envy comes dressed in a great coat, and his sleeves are like those of a friar. He bites his lips with suppressed anger, his clenched fist reveals vindictiveness, and this unhealthy emotional attitude has affected his digestion. He confesses the sin of backbiting against his neighbor; yet when he meets him in the marketplace, he greets him like a friend because he is afraid of him. "But had I mastery and might," he says, "I would murder him at once!" (A V 84). In church he asks Christ to bring sorrow on the thief who took his bowl and his torn sheet, and gazes enviously on the new clothes worn by a fortunate couple in the sanctuary. When they suffer losses, he laughs; when they prosper, he weeps and wails. Thus I live loveless, he confesses, like a wretched dog, my breast swelling from the bitterness of my gall. No patent medicine seems to do my system any good: if confession should help, it would be a miracle. His confessor, Repentance, seizes this opportunity to urge him to mend his ways: "Sorrow for sin saveth very many." Playing on two meanings of the word sorrow (remorse and enviousness), the wretched sinner concludes (A V 104–05):

> "I am sorry," said Envy, "I am seldom otherwise,
> For it makes me angry that I may get no revenge."

Next comes the gaunt figure of Covetousness, dressed in a threadbare coat, whose confession is an inventory of the practices of Guile in borough: as an apprentice he learned to lie and weigh falsely; when his master sent him to the fair with his merchandise, it would never have been sold in seven years had not the "grace of guile" gone with him. "Then I signed up with the drapers," he says, "to learn my Donet (grammar): how to stretch out the cloth until ten or twelve yards measured thirteen. My wife used deceptive practices both in weaving and in brewing: her name is Rose the retailer, and she has been a huckster these eleven years. But now I repent all this: my wife and I shall go on pilgrimage to Walsingham, and pray the true cross to bring me out of debt."

Gluttony is on his way to confession when he is hailed by Betty the brewster and invited into the tavern for a drink. Soon he is engaged in a drinking contest with a small army of disreputable companions, and ends up so drunk that he can scarcely make it home. Stumbling on the threshold, he passes out completely, leaving his wife and a serving girl with the unpleasant task of dragging him to his bed. After sleeping through the weekend, he wakes up, wipes his eyes and asks, "Where is the cup?" But when his wife rebukes him for his wickedness, he is ashamed and vows to fast on Fridays.

Sloth is the final sin to step forward, unless we count Robert the robber as a separate member of the group. If we set aside the possibility of scribal error, it would appear to me that Sloth *is* Robert the robber, meaning that a life of thievery is the result of sloth—a perverse unwillingness to work hard in the normal way. This would explain Sloth's vow to restore his "wicked winnings." It is not the most common view of the sin, but, as we have noted, the poet often gives traditional concepts his own emphasis. The confession ends with Robert's prayer that Christ will forgive him as he did the penitent thief on the cross, and his tearful promise to reform his life. This repentance then merges with that of the folk in the field (A V 251–54):

> Thousands of people then thronged together,
> Weeping and wailing for their wicked deeds,
> Praying to Christ and to His pure mother,
> For grace to seek Truth, if God grant that they may!

Piers and the Plowing of the Half Acre

We have been shown what is wrong with society, and we have seen the repentance of the folk in the field. Now we are to meet the hero of the poem, Piers the plowman himself, who is the poet's answer to Lady Meed: a man of integrity. There are those among modern interpreters of the poem who would tell us that Piers is in some sense fallible, or that his way to Truth stands in need of improvement. On the contrary, Piers is intended as a model for us all, even when he appears to be confessing himself a sinner, and the path to Truth which he offers is derived from basic Christian doctrine, sufficient in every way for salvation. If there is any hint to the contrary, it is to be found in the later revisions of the poem.

Before introducing his hero, the poet cannot resist playing on our expectations of a pilgrimage by introducing a conventional pilgrim of the type already satirized in the prologue. He is dressed like a pagan—that is, in imitation of Near Eastern clothing to suggest that he has perhaps just come from Arabia. He has decorated himself with the emblems of famous shrines: ampules from Canterbury, signs of Sinai, shells of Galicia, and the cross keys and vernicle of Rome. When the folk ask him where he has been, he tells them he has seen Sinai, the Holy Sepulcher, Bethlehem, Babylon, Armenia, Alexandria, and many other places. But when they ask him how to find Truth, he confesses complete ignorance.

At this opportune moment, Piers the plowman puts forth his head and offers to guide the pilgrims to Saint Truth. I know him well, says Piers, and I will show you the way. When they offer him money for his services, Piers angrily refuses it, and proceeds to describe the way to Truth by means of an allegorical map made up of the Ten Commandments, as well as humility, conscience, the great commandment (Matt. 22:37–40), and various requisite virtues. He who follows these directions will come finally to the celestial court of Truth, whose moat is of Mercy, walls of Wit to keep out Will (desire), battlements of faith, and the roof made of love and humility. Truth's tower rises to the sun. The gatekeeper is Grace and his assistant is Amend-you. When you get there, give him this password: I performed the penance enjoined by the priest, and am sorry for my sins. And if Grace permits you to enter, you shall see Truth sitting in your heart. Let no pride keep you from loving him and keeping his commandments. Remember, anyone who is kin to the seven sisters (seven virtues) who keep the posterns will be assured of admission; unless you are related to at least one of these seven, you may find it difficult to get in. At this news a cutpurse, an apeward, and a waferer disclaim any such kinship, and the latter vows that if he knew that to be a fact, he would not go one foot farther, "for any friar's preaching." But Piers hastens to reassure them that Mercy, along with her Son, always stands ready to admit them through grace.

The folk cry for a guide, and Piers agrees to lead them—except that he must first plow a half acre beside the highway. The women are set to work spinning, weaving, and sewing. When a knight offers to plow, Piers thanks him for proffering himself so humbly, but says that he will work for them both and asks only that the knight defend the faith, keep law and order, and hunt down predators that break into his croft. As an afterthought Piers cautions the knight not to oppress tenants, mistreat bondmen, or waste time and money on bawdy entertainers. The knight agrees to all this, and Piers dresses for the pilgrimage, hanging a hopper (seed basket) at his neck instead of a scrip (traveler's wallet), suggesting that Piers' pilgrimage is not to be the conventional kind. I shall provide food for everyone who helps me, announces Piers, except for Jake the juggler, Janette of the stews, and Robin the ribald for his raunchy words. He then makes his will (as if in preparation for a journey), and the plowing of the half acres begins.

At high prime (6 a.m.) Piers lets the plow stand, and finds that there are some sitting in the alehouse, helping him plow only with a "hey, trolly-lolly!" (A VII 108). Enraged, Piers threatens to deny them his food, even if this means starvation, unless they get to work. In response to this outburst, some plead sickness or disability, and Waster and his Breton companion threaten to fight, warning Piers that they will eat his food whether he likes it or not. When the knight's official warning to Waster is ignored, Piers as a last resort sends after Hunger, who assaults Waster and the Breton so violently that the plowman has to intervene to save their lives. Seeing this, the ill and handicapped are suddenly cured (A VII 175–80):

> A horde of hermits took hold of their spades,
> And dug dirt and dung to drive Hunger out.
> The blind and the bedridden were cured by the thousands,
> Who feigned blindness and broken legs by the highway;
> Hunger had healed them with a hot cake.
> The limbs of lame men were suddenly lithe. . . .

But what about the morality of threatening starvation to get people to work? These men are my brothers, says Piers to Hunger, for whom Christ died, and Truth taught me to love them: what do you advise? Hunger responds: those that appear physically strong ("bold beggars") should be fed with beans, and if they complain, tell them to go to work and their diet will improve; but victims of genuine misfortune, the needy and naked, should be loved and supported with food or money. It is for this reason that the gospel says, "Make to yourselves friends of the mammon of unrighteousness" (Luke 16:9).

Piers wants to be sure that it is safe to follow Hunger's teaching, so he asks: "May I do without sin what you have said?" (A VII 214). Hunger responds with a shower of biblical texts: "In the sweat of thy face shalt thou eat bread" (Gen. 3:19); "The sluggard will not plow by reason of the cold, therefore he shall beg in harvest, and have nothing" (Prov. 20:3); and the parable of the talents (Matt. 25:14–20). It is only natural, he adds, that everyone work at some job such as teaching, tilling, or working with his hands. Christ himself commends both the active and the contemplative life (Luke 10:38–42), although the Psalter contains a special blessing for those who work with their hands (Ps. 128:2). For the record, Hunger seems to concede obliquely that Christ commended the contemplative life (Mary) over the active life (Martha) while nevertheless leaving an impression that the Bible singles out the working man for particular praise.

In a final and unexpected request, Piers asks Hunger for medical advice: some of my servants are sick at times, he says, taking off from work as much as a week because of the stomach-ache. If you want to be healthy, advises Hunger, here are some rules: never drink until you have had some dinner; do not eat until Hunger sends you his sauce to appeal to your palate; keep some until supper, and sit not too long at table, but arise before Appetite has eaten his fill. Let not Sir Surfeit sit at your table. Follow these rules, and I dare say Physic shall sell his furred hood to buy food and learn to labor on the land. There are more liars than leeches—may our Lord amend them—they make men die prematurely with their potions!

Piers receives Hunger's advice with enthusiastic approval, and grants him permission to leave. But Hunger will not go until he has been fed, and his appetite is so enormous that nothing satisfies him until harvest time when the new grain comes to market: then they feed him so full that he falls asleep. Whereupon Waster immediately quits work, and beggars eat only the best white bread and drink brown ale. Day laborers deign not to dine on day-old vegetables, and demand fresh meat or fried fish, cooked exactly to taste. Unless they have higher wages they complain, bewailing the time they became workmen, and cursing the king and his council for designing such laws as the Statute of Laborers. But while Hunger was their master, observes the poet, no one would chide or strive against the statute, so stern was his glance. Although it is clear that our author has a high regard for the role of the laboring man, he has no inclination whatever to give them preferential treatment. They have no right to take advantage of the special circumstances of the period following the plague to extort high wages from the landowners. The passus concludes with a threatening prophecy (A VII 302–07):

> I warn you workmen, earn while you may;
> For Hunger hitherward hastens to return;
> He shall awaken through water to punish wasters;
> Before five years are finished, such famine shall arise,
> Through floods and foul weather, that fruit trees shall fail,
> And so says Saturn, who sends you this warning.

Truth's Pardon: The End of the Visio

The author of the A text seems to take a special delight in confounding our expectations. In the episode of Lady Meed we witness elaborate plans for a wedding that never takes place; at the appearance of the good plowman we are led to expect a literal pilgrimage that does not occur; and now, at the climactic moment of the entire *Visio*, we are presented with a pardon that is no pardon at all. The distinctive blend of irony and anger in this scene has left generations of interpreters puzzled, but oncc the reader is attuned to the poet's penchant for practical jokes, the meaning of his conclusion becomes painfully clear.

Because of the famine predicted by Saturn, Truth sends Piers a pardon, with a message instructing him to stay at home (that is, forget the proposed pilgrimage) and plow his land. The indulgence he sends is in the form of a pardon *a pena et a culpa* (from punishment and guilt), despite the fact that such certificates were not supposed to offer exemption from the guilt of sin. This generous pardon is offered to Piers and his heirs, and all who help him with his work, whatever their position in society. The poet then proceeds through the ranks, indicating how each group may or may not partake of the benefits of this pardon.

Kings and knights who defend Holy Church and govern the people are permitted to pass quickly through purgatory into paradise. Bishops who bless, and know both laws, observing the one and teaching men the other, who preach to their parsons the peril of sin, and how they are to save their flocks–such bishops have as full a pardon as the apostles, and will sit with them in a place of honor on Judgment Day. Merchants, in the margin (as an afterthought), are given many years remission of punishment, but the pope will not grant it them *a pena et a culpa*, because they fail to close down their shops on holy days and swear in God's name that their goods are of high quality when they know better. But Truth sends them a special set of instructions, assuring them that they might buy and sell with a good conscience, as long as they use their profits to support hospitals, repair roads and bridges, provide dowries for maidens, subsidies for poor widows, scholarships for students or apprentices, and support for the religious orders. If they do these things, Truth promises to send Saint Michael himself to escort them to heaven when they die. As long as they avoid usury, avarice, false oaths, and guile in their transactions and follow a strict path, they have nothing to fear. Hearing this, merchants were merry and wept for joy, and gave Will expensive clothing as a reward for thus copying their clause (A VIII 43–44).

Men of law had least share in the pardon of Truth, because they are all educated, and can't plead ignorance of the Psalter: "Lord, who shall abide in thy tabernacle? Who shall dwell in thy holy hill? . . . He that . . . taketh (not) reward against the innocent" (Ps. 15:1, 5). Lawyers should receive their income from princes and prelates, and they should not take so much as one penny from poor people. But he who speaks for the poor and innocent without demanding money, and who gives him the benefit of his legal knowledge purely for love of the Lord, there is no devil that can harm him at all on his death day, for he shall be safely delivered unto the holy hill of the Lord as the Psalter promises. For there are three things that cannot be bought or sold: water, wind, and wit, all of them gifts of God, granted for our common good. The man who takes meed from a poor man for pleading his case in court will get very little pardon in purgatory, I believe, says Truth. You barristers and lawyers, you know whether I am lying or not! Since you know it is true, you'd do well to take my advice.

All true laborers who work with their hands, living with humble hearts in love and in law, have the same absolution that was sent to Piers. But beggars are not in the pardon, unless there is a genuine reason for them to beg. False beggars defraud the truly needy, and beguile the giver against his will. They live loveless and lawless lives, scorning marriage and coupling with women like animals. Then they take their bastard child and break its back or some other bone in order to use it as an object of pity in their begging. That is why you see so many cripples in this miserable group. Those who live like this may well dread the time when they depart this life. But the old and helpless, women with child who cannot work, the blind and bedridden, with broken members, who take their mischief meekly, have as full a pardon as the plowman himself. For love of their humble hearts, our Lord has granted them their penance and their purgatory upon this pure earth.

It is hard to miss the deep emotion in the concluding lines of this pardon, but at the same time we should not lose sight of what has been accomplished. The wealthy and powerful have been reminded forcefully of their responsibilities, lawyers have been warned of the doom that awaits them if they do not change, while laborers, the poor, and the handicapped have been assured of their salvation. Would it have been possible for anyone in the poet's audience to have seen an actual pardon containing such provisions? Certainly not. Those who obey the conditions of this "pardon" have also been obedient to the law of God, and therefore have no need of any pardon whatsoever. Indeed they will have brought upon themselves *no punishment and no guilt,* and will thus receive in full what had seemed in the beginning a pardon that made excessive claims. Truth here employs the same kind of irony as that used earlier by Reason when he promised to show mercy at a time when mercy will no longer be needed (A IV 100–131).

At this dramatic moment a priest offers to read the pardon for Piers and translate it into English. The Dreamer, looking over their shoulder, could see that the text consisted of two lines only (A VIII 94a):

> *Et qui bona egerunt ibunt in vitam eternam;*
> *Qui vero mala, in ignem eternum.*

When the priest sees this, he exclaims, "Peter! No pardon is here" (A

VIII 95), and proceeds to give a translation: Those who do well will go into eternal life, but those who do evil will go into eternal fire. Of course the priest is correct: this is no pardon. It is in fact a deliberately chosen extract from the Athanasian Creed, which is binding on all Christians. Establish this clause in the minds and hearts of worshipers, and all the elaborate machinery of penance devised by the medieval church will become superfluous. The abuses that have grown up in connection with the employment of "real" pardons show that Lady Meed has found her way to the heart of the confessional. At one stroke, Truth cuts through the penitential red tape and confounds the literal-minded priest.

On the other hand, Piers completely understands Truth's message, and accepts it. But this message is not a "doctrine" to which one merely gives "assent"; it is a divine warning that ought to produce fear and trembling in the listener. And this is precisely the response that it elicits from the plowman. His anger with the priest, expressed in his tearing of the pretended pardon, quickly gives way to a penitential confession of faith (Ps. 23:4) and a vow to be less anxious for his bodily welfare (Matt. 6:25). In this brief confession, Piers both demonstrates the uselessness of indulgences and shows us the correct response to Truth's message. Isaiah called himself a man of unclean lips (Isa. 6:5); Job despised himself and repented in dust and ashes (Job 42:5); Piers confesses an excessive concern for his daily bread, and promises in future to show more faith in Christ's assurances in the Sermon on the Mount.

If Piers finds something in himself that needs reforming, the rest of us must surely search our hearts. But the priest who offered to interpret the pardon is apparently oblivious of the spiritual issues now vibrant in the air, and can only express a condescending surprise at the scriptural knowledge that Piers reveals in his confession. "By Peter!" he exclaims, "you have a little learning; who taught you your letters?" (A VIII 115). This precipitates a quarrel between the plowman and the priest, which causes the Dreamer to awaken and find himself alone on Malvern hills.

Traditionally in medieval vision literature, the poet disclaims responsibility for his dream and encourages the reader to draw his own conclusions about its significance. The author of the A text follows this convention, but leaves little doubt how we are to interpret his poem. I have thought about this dream many times, he says, wondering if it might be true. Cato says we should pay no attention to dreams, but the Bible, in stories of Joseph and Daniel, tells of dreams that came true. Many times at midnight, when men should be sleeping, I think about Piers the plowman, what kind of pardon he had, and how the priest impugned it, all by pure reason. And I concluded that doing well (Dowel) surpassed indulgences. Dowel will be honorably received on the Day of Judgment, and surpasses all the pardons of Saint Peter's church. He goes on to concede, lest anyone accuse him of heresy, that he does not doubt the pope's authority to distribute such indulgences, or his power to bind and loose (Matt. 16:19). But he insists that in moments of crisis it is safer ultimately to trust in Dowel than in pardons or masses said on behalf of your soul.

The conclusion to the *Visio* has a message that should be of considerable comfort to the poor and helpless, since it is only the rich and powerful who can afford the price of most indulgences and the singing of masses for the dead. To the latter group the poet addresses a final warning: I advise you rich who trust on such masses not to be any bolder to break the Ten Commandments! And especially you magistrates, mayors, and judges, who have the wealth of this world and are considered wise, and can afford pardons and papal bulls: beware of Doomsday, when you will be required to account for all your actions. A sackful of pardons will do you no good there; unless Dowel help you, I wouldn't give a crumb for your patent! Then, in a closing prayer, the poet asks God to give us all grace to lead such lives that on Doomsday Dowel will testify that we obeyed the commandments.

The *Visio* thus ends with a vindication of the Plowman and his way of life, measured against the sins and pretensions of church and state. In the process we have been introduced to a new allegorical figure, Dowel, embodying the good life as lived in accordance with Truth's pardon. And it is Dowel, as we shall see, that provides the point of departure for the *Vita*, the final section of the poem.

The Life of Dowel, Dobet, and Dobest

The ostensible purpose of the Dreamer is to set out in quest of the good life—the life lived in accordance with Truth. He does this by consulting various mental faculties and aids to his education: Thought, Wit, Study, Clergy (learning), and Scripture. Each of these is to give the Dreamer his or her definition of the kind of life that will lead to salvation, as implied in Truth's pardon. When he has completed his education, the Dreamer should finally be able to provide us with a reliable definition of the way of Truth. Such will be our expectation, that is, if we have forgotten about the poet's perverse inclination to play tricks, to let us cultivate a set of false expectations, as he did with the marriage of Meed, the pilgrimage of Piers, and the pardon of Truth.

In the first place, we quickly discover that there is no real progression from one spokesman to the next: no one definition is necessarily an improvement over another. Furthermore, the triad into which the concept of doing well is now divided refers, not to any single pattern of life more or less well-imitated, but rather to three ranks of society that the poet wishes to examine: Dowel stands for the common people, Dobet the clergy (both secular and regular), and Dobest the episcopate. The standards applied to these ranks (good, better, best) merely reflect the escalating pressure for moral behavior in relation to positions of increasing responsibility. With this arrangement we can see that the commons, though much is demanded of them, are in a less vulnerable position than the other two groups. The clergy ought to lead more exemplary lives, and of course bishops ought to be better than priests.

Thus the quest of the Dreamer turns out to be not a search for something, but an opportunity to expose the shortcomings of society when measured against the standards of Truth. This means that the Dreamer's questions are not those of a troubled author genuinely seeking answers, but rather opening sallies in a debate designed to reveal sin, corruption, and hypocrisy. Interpreters of *Piers Plowman* have long insisted–so long and so eloquently that it seems almost perverse to disagree–that the *Vita* expresses the theological uncertainties of the poet. Yet I must insist, at least as far as the A version is concerned, that we will find it difficult, if not impossible, to understand the *Vita* unless we realize that it is filled with irony, satire, and even comedy: ingredients that are the opposite of what we should expect from an author who is unsure of himself. And readers of the *Visio* should not be surprised when we discover that most of the author's barbs are aimed at Dobet, the life of the clergy. It was a priest who sneered at the plowman's knowledge of Scripture, and we are not to be allowed to forget this. It is no exaggeration to say that a main purpose of the *Vita* is to prove that the path of learning is *not* the way to salvation.

The Dreamer roams in search of Dowel, asking repeatedly of folk that he meets who this man might be and where he might be found. At length he encounters a pair of friars, who insist that Dowel dwells with them, but the Dreamer does not seem convinced by their elaborate distinction between venial and deadly sin. Bidding them a polite farewell, he comes to a wood, leans against a linden tree, and falls asleep to the sound of the birds.

In his dream a large man approaches him, looking much like himself, and calls the Dreamer by name. "Who are you," said I, "who know my right name?" (A IX 63). I am Thought, the man replies: I've been following you for seven years–haven't you seen me before? The Dreamer asks him where Dowel lives, and Thought responds by defining the triad as "three fair virtues." Dowel is meek and mild in speech, true of his tongue and his two hands, and earns his living by labor–honest, sober, and upright. Dobet does likewise, but in addition he is as low as a lamb, generous, and lovely of speech. In some cases he joins the religious orders and makes himself a friend of the mammon of unrighteousness (Luke 16:9), glossing the Bible to show that what he is doing is right, and preaching on the text "Suffer fools gladly, seeing ye yourselves are wise" (2 Cor. 11:19). Dobest is above both, and bears a bishop's crosier, with a hook at one end to hold men in good life; it also has a point to strike down the wicked who may be intending to harm Dowel.

In this paraphrase I have tried to indicate that these opening definitions are quite simple, and yet the definition of Dobet already contains a hint of the hostility that is to emerge in later characterizations of this group. The clergy are *supposed* to be humble and generous with what they have, but the glossing of the mammon verse from Luke by the religious orders is suspect, and the poet turns some of Saint Paul's irony in 2 Corinthians 11:19 against the condescending preachers who invoke him in their sermons. This kind of two-edged sword is common in the *Vita*. But Thought can also be perfectly serious, as he is in this often misunderstood description of the relationship of the three members of the triad (A IX 90–96):

> And as Do-well and Do-better agreed together,
> They have crowned one king to keep peace among all,
> So that if Do-well and Do-better disobeyed Do-best,
> And were rebellious to his bidding and bold to do evil,
> Then should the king come and cast them in prison,
> And put them there in penance, without pity or grace;
> And unless Do-best intercede, abide there forever.

This passage takes up one aspect of the relation of church and state in order to show that the royal power is to be used when necessary to give bishops a means of disciplining both the commons and the clergy. In short, the king is the bishop's enforcer. He is to rule by the advice of his council, and with the assent of all ranks of society (A IX 97–100). When the Dreamer expresses dissatisfaction with this definition, Thought refers him to Wit, our next spokesman.

Wit is the resident psychologist of the *Vita*, and his initial response to the Dreamer's question is a classic description of the nature and destiny of man, cast in allegorical form. Dowel (mankind) dwells in a castle (the body), and is responsible, along with Dobet and Dobest, for defending Lady Anima (the soul) against the schemes of a proud chevalier of France, Prince of this World—the Devil (John 16:11). The constable of the castle is Inwit (conscience), who with his five sons (approximating the five senses) is charged with defending the Lady until Kind (God/Nature) sends for her and takes over the responsibility for her defense himself (that is, after the death of the body).

If we keep in mind the poet's prophetic stance, it should come as no surprise to discover that Wit's psychology is fundamentally optimistic. He points out to the Dreamer that God created man in his own image, and consequently provided him with all the means necessary to lead a good life. Thus man has been given Inwit (conscience) as a guide to both body and soul, and a restraint against excesses. The home of Inwit is the head, where he is in a firm position to govern, unless blood becomes stronger than brain (emotion overcomes reason). When this happens, then Inwit is bound or helpless, and the person runs wild. Such is the case with infants, fools (madmen), or drunkards who pour ale in their heads until Inwit is drowned. In the latter instance the result is that the Devil gains power over their souls. But in the case of infants or fools the Devil has no power because of any mistakes that they make. As for infants, it is up to parents and friends to steer them away from wantonness while they are young; and if they are destitute, then Holy Church is responsible for keeping them from folly and providing subsistence until they grow wiser and are able to care for themselves.

Thus it should be evident that every person of understanding is given sovereignty over himself to protect his soul, and when he passes childhood, to clear himself of any charge, and save himself from sin: "For whether he does well or ill, the wit is his own" (A X 75). When we look back at the friar's sermon near the beginning of the *Vita*, we can see that by comparision Wit's attitude toward sin is absolutely uncompromising: if the just man sinneth seven times in a day (Prov. 24:16), so much the worse for him. And it should be clear which side the author takes on this point: only Wit's psychology can prepare us to meet the absolute demands of Truth. If we follow his guidance, vices can be destroyed, and "sin has no power" to strike root in our hearts.

Having presented his views on the mechanism of the soul and its relation to the body, Wit now launches into his own definition of the triad. Dowel is fear of God, Dobet is fear of the rod (of correction!), and Dobest is humility. Not surprisingly, Wit focuses on *attitude*, but it is clear that the groups in society are the same: commons, clergy, and episcopate. For each rank he has a biblical text. Dowel: "The fear of the Lord is the beginning of wisdom" (Ps. 111:10); Dobet: "Thy rod and thy staff they comfort me" (Ps. 23:4); and Dobest: "He that humbleth himself shall be exalted" (Luke 14:11). The rod of punishment and the staff of support belong to a venerable tradition of exegesis of the Twenty-third Psalm; but it is significant to note here that the assignment of a rod of punishment to the clergy is typical of what we may expect from this poet.

Was there any "upward mobility" in medieval society? Indeed there was, and it was made possible largely by the Church, which drew on all ranks, including the commons, in its quest for candidates for the priesthood. But our poet seems to have an aversion to this, or at least to the kind of person he saw striving for ecclesiastical preferment. This comes out in a digression following the definition of Dobet. If your conscience tells you that you are doing well, he says, do not ever seek to do better. As long as you live in accordance with God's word, do not become angry because of anything men say about you. Stay in your place, and do not seek to go higher: for if you do, your humility may give way to pride. A trodden stone gathers no moss (aimed at those who play the game of musical monasteries); and the jack of all trades is master of none (ambition in the marketplace). Paul warned us against running about: "Let every man abide in the same calling wherein he was called" (1 Cor. 7:20). Whether you are a married man or a monk or a canon, live in such a way that you will be blessed for your steadfast life, even if you were a beggar. Do not complain against God, and be satisfied with your position.

In summarizing his definitions, Wit likens the flourishing of society to the growth of a flower. Just as a rose that is red and sweet, he says, grows out of a ragged root (the commons) and a rough briar (the clergy!), so Dobest (bishops) springs from Dobet and Dowel. The anticlerical nature of the image is clear, but we should also note that the commons are the root of society, and thus absolutely essential to its development. This is in sharp contrast to the viewpoint destined to appear later in the B version, where the priesthood is the root, and the rest of society flower, leaf, and fruit (B XV 97–100).

Although it seems at times in the A text as if the common man is being readied for a messianic role, this never becomes explicit, because the poet is painfully aware of the shortcomings of the people. They are exploited, and this makes him angry; but a certain amount of their suffering is self-inflicted. This is made clear in the remainder of this passus by Wit's dissection of the institution of marriage. Dowel is made up of wedded folk, and "in wedlock the world stands" (A X 129). One is reminded of the Wife of Bath's triumphant observation (CT III 71–72):

> And certes, if there were no seed ysowe,
> Virginitẹe, thanne wherof sholde it growe?

But Wit is engaged in making a serious point: the flourishing of society is absolutely dependent on the soundness of the institution of marriage.

Wit traces the problems afflicting marriage in his time back to the Fall (Gen. 3:16), specifically to the birth of Cain (citing Ps. 7:14), and the subsequent intermarriage of the children of Seth and Cain despite God's warning against that. Indeed, God's purpose in sending the Flood was to wipe out that evil generation. But if we look around us, we can see that Cain's offspring are alive and well in the wretched marriages of today. Some marry for greed: a young girl is betrothed to an old man, or a wealthy widow is married for her money when she is of such an age that she will never bear a child unless it be in her arms. Since the pestilence, many a joyless couple have jangled in bed, and the only offspring they have are foul words hurled at each other (A X 184–87). You can be sure that none of them will win the side of bacon in Dunmow (a prize for the couple that has gone a whole year without quarreling).

In conclusion Wit urges all Christians to exclude covetousness from marriage. Let virgins marry virgins, widows wed widowers, and thank God for any incidental benefits that may come from the wedding. It goes without saying that fornication and adultery are to be strictly avoided.

Such sins have practical consequences: their bastard offspring grow up to become loveless wanderers and wasters who, without God's grace, will end up going to hell. Summarizing the triad, Wit says that Dowel is to fear, Dobet is to suffer, and Dobest has a disciplinary function: to abase the proud.

The final passus of the *Vita* opens with the sudden appearance of Wit's wife, Dame Study, who launches into a brilliant monologue that provides both comic relief and satiric thrust. It is comic to discover that Wit, having just delivered an authoritative critique of marriage, has such an obstreperous wife; and it is her reckless assumption that the Dreamer is a quibbling intellectual that provides the basis for a sharp attack on learning.

Don't cast your pearls before swine, says Dame Study; they prefer slops to all the jewels that grow in paradise! I mean those who would rather have land and lordship than all the wisdom of Solomon. Indeed wisdom nowadays is not worth a straw unless it is brushed up with covetousness and used to frustrate justice. Those who can do this are called into council, and are treated as lords when in fact they are serving the devil. "Wherefore do the wicked live, become old, yea, are mighty in power?" (Job 21:7). Meanwhile he who has holy writ in his mouth is pushed aside to make room for professional entertainers. Minstrels know very well that if their stories are not mostly harlotry they will not receive so much as a groat, whether their audience includes king, knight, or canon of Saint Paul's! Lechery and loose tales, gluttony and great oaths, these are games nowadays!

But if these clerks or laymen do speak of Christ, during dinner, when minstrels are quiet, then they talk of the Trinity, how Two slew the Third, and offer a presumption to "prove" the truth. Thus they talk drivel on the dais, and gnaw God in their gorge, when their guts are full. But the poor man may cry at the gate, trembling for hunger and cold, and no one takes him in; instead he is driven out like a dog and told to go elsewhere. He who shares thus with the poor has little love for the Lord who gave him all that he enjoys. If it were not for the fact that poor men are more merciful than the rich, many beggars would go to bed without food. God is much in the throats of these great masters, but among poor men are found his mercy and his works. To find the truly devout, you must go to the hinterlands (Ps. 132:6): "Lo, we heard of it at Ephratah: we found it in the fields of the wood."

In the person of Dame Study, the poet has perhaps allowed himself to voice an extreme position, but there is a sincerity and an urgency in this speech that can scarcely be denied. Indeed the frequency with which the later versions refer back to this passage (in tones of anguish rather than anger, as in A) suggests that Study's fulminations had a profound impact on the reviser. In her rage, Dame Study speaks with utter seriousness and with profound disrespect for the high-ranking victims of her criticism. Deceiving friars have dreamed up questions, she continues, to please proud men and defile our faith when they sit at their feasts. Now every boy is bold, if he be rich, to talk about the Trinity to enhance his reputation, and to raise such questions as: why would God allow the serpent into Paradise? But Saint Augustine long ago had the answer to such quibblers, warning them not to be wiser than is fitting. Everything happens in accordance with God's will, whatever we may think!

At the height of her indignation, Dame Study now turns her attention back to the Dreamer. And now comes a clod, she says scornfully, who would pick my brain about a distinction between Dowel and Dobet—now let him go deaf! Unless he first live to the minutest detail the life of Dowel, I dare say he will never Dobet, even if Dobest were to drag him by the heels! In response to this outburst, the Dreamer begs Wit to intercede, but the embarrassed and apparently henpecked husband can only laugh and bow and gesture to indicate that he will have to ask her for mercy himself.

When the Dreamer kneels obediently before her, asking only to be told what Dowel is, Dame Study suddenly turns gentle. I appreciate your meekness, young man, she says, and so I shall direct you to my cousin Clergy (learning) and his wife Scripture. This she proceeds to do, using one of those allegorical maps of which the author is very fond (compare A VI 47–123). But before bidding him farewell, the Dame provides an inventory of subjects that go with a life of study, accompanied by her own colorful opinions. Concerning theology, for example, she confesses that it has often vexed her, because the more she looked into it, the more obscure it seemed. It is certainly not a science to be subtle about, and the only reason she tolerates it is that it exalts love above everything else. And when love is lord, grace will never be lacking.

With the blessing of Dame Study, the Dreamer now follows her directions to the house of Clergy and Scripture, where he is warmly welcomed. Wasting no time, the Dreamer asks about the triad. Clergy replies with what is by now the conventional definition: Dowel is the life of laborers, Dobet the clergy (who lead a life of charitable aid to others and harmony among themselves!), and Dobest is prince over God's people, to preach and to chastise. There is no appreciable advance in this over earlier definitions, but the reason is not hard to find: the author is about to ignite an argument by means of which the poem will be brought to its conclusion. In the *Visio*, we recall, the dream ends with an argument between Piers and the priest (A VIII 95–126); the *Vita* will end in a "dispute" betwen the Dreamer and Scripture. The difference is that whereas there was a profound disagreement betwen the plowman and the priest, the row between the Dreamer and Scripture is patently contrived to allow a final satirical thrust at the monastic orders, as well as at the wealthy and powerful. Throughout the dispute, the Dreamer is speaking tongue in cheek.

The opening for this argument is provided by Scripture, whose definition of Dobet turns into a tirade against the religious orders. Dobet is endowed, she remarks, for the sake of poor men. I speak of the truly religious, not those who leap over the land to confess ladies (the friars). Gregory the Great rightly said that a monk out of his cloister is like a fish out of water. But nowadays Religion has become a rider, a roamer of streets, a leader of lovedays, and a buyer of land. He trots on a palfrey from town to town, wears a dagger, and swears like a lord. This is the life of those that should live with Dobet, and even worse, if I were to tell all.

At this point the Dreamer interrupts: I thought that kings and knights represented the triad, since Christ himself said, "Princes sit in Moses' seat" (cf. Matt. 23:2). This misquoting of the gospel, where it is the scribes and the Pharisees, not princes, who sit in the seat of Moses, conveniently allows Scripture to point out that the rich and powerful have no special privileges in the eyes of God, and that indeed the poor have the promise of heaven while the wealthy do not. We are already quite aware that this is a sentiment with which the Dreamer strongly agrees, so that unless we are attuned to the poet's irony we will be surprised to discover that the Dreamer proceeds to attack Scripture's position in the manner of a disputatious clerk.

On the contrary, says the Dreamer to Scripture, I can prove that rich men *are* saved (Mark 16:16): "He that believeth and is baptized shall be saved." Patiently Scripture responds that this verse refers to special circumstances, as in the baptism of converts from other faiths, whereas Christians have a common heritage of doctrine that must be obeyed before salvation can be assured. For example, continues Scripture, launching into her *finale*, there is the command to love God and your neighbor. This means that Christians should be kind to one another, and also help the heathen, in hope of improving them: certainly God never commanded us to kill them (as in the crusades), for he says himself in the Decalogue, "Thou shalt not kill," and elsewhere, "Vengeance is mine; I will repay, saith the Lord" (Rom. 12:19). the *Vita* thus ends with a sharp thrust at one of the great causes adopted by the warrior class, and widely approved by medieval society. If God indeed opposes the crusades, a radical reassessment of what constitutes the good life is certainly in order. Having thus disrupted our conventional notions of piety, the author leaves us to ponder the meaning of his dream.

But as in the case of the *Visio*, we are given a closing meditation by the Dreamer designed to make clear what the poet wants us to learn from the *Vita*. And yet I am never the nearer, says the Dreamer, for all my walking, to a true knowledge of Dowel. For whatever I do in this life, I have been predestined either for salvation or damnation. Consider the cases of Solomon and Aristotle: who did better than they? Yet all Holy Church maintains that they are in hell! And this despite the fact that learned men now use their words to guide us to Dowel. But it may be unwise of me to follow their wisdom, considering what happened to them: I might end up in hell myself!

On Good Friday, he continues, a felon was saved who had lived as a thief all his life. Merely because he confessed to Christ on the cross, he had salvation sooner than Saint John the Baptist, Adam, Isaiah, or any of the prophets who had lain with Lucifer many long years. A *robber* had remission sooner than all of them! Who did worse than Mary Magdalene, David, slayer of Uriah, or Paul, who participated in the killing of Christians? yet there is none so surely established in heaven as these, who lived such wicked lives when they were in the world.

The reader, who has by this time become familiar with the author's tendency to tease us with false expectations, will recognize, of course, that we are being treated to one more example of his perversity. As far as the Dreamer and the poet are concerned, these instances are not real problems, but ridiculous examples of theological impasse. They are what happens when, as Dame Study warned, you seek to be wiser than is fitting. Having treated us to this parade of absurdities, the Dreamer now makes the moral of the poem explicit.

And yet I have forgotten the teaching of my five wits, he says, namely that Christ never did commend learning. On the contrary he said: "When you are questioned by princes or *priests of the law*, have no fear to answer them, for I shall give you the grace of the Holy Ghost to answer them all" (cf. Mark 13:11, 13). This is a somewhat free paraphrase of the gospel, and it is worth noting that for "ruler and kings" the author has substituted "princes *and priests*," thus reminding us of that confrontation between Piers and the priest in the *Visio*, where the unlettered plowman is given the apparently inspired ability to refute the legalistic priest from Scripture.

A final, clinching paraphrase of Saint Augustine caps the poet's denunciation of learning, and brings the *Vita* to an end (A XI 297–303):

> None are more tempted from the true faith,
> Than are these great scholars who study many books,
> Nor are any sooner saved nor more steadfast in conscience,
> Than poor people such as plowmen and penniless shepherds.
> Cobblers and shoemakers, such ignorant dolts,
> Pierce with a prayer the palace of heaven,
> Without penance at their parting, pass into high bliss!

Learned commentators in modern times have been understandably reluctant to interpret the close of the A *Vita* as a decisive denunciation of learning, and their reluctance may be due to more than a personal commitment to the advancement of learning: for the reviser does everything in his power to refute this conclusion in the B and C versions of the poem. But we are still more than twenty years away from the B version, and it is well to remind ourselves that however hard it may be for us to swallow the lesson of the *Vita*, John Ball and his comrades had no such problem. Concerning the attitude of the rebels toward literate members of society, the chronicler Walsingham had this to say (Dobson, 364): "It was dangerous enough to be known as a clerk, but especially dangerous if an ink-pot should be found at one's elbow: such men scarcely or ever escaped from the hands of the rebels." Nowhere do I mean to imply that the author of *Piers Plowman* (A) would have sanctioned the violence of the peasants in 1381. But in many respects his attitude did pose a threat to the established order, and pointed a dagger at the heart of the system governing both church and state. His dream of a golden age proved very attractive to the rebel leadership, and meant nothing but trouble for those who stood in the way of its fulfillment.

The Peasants' Revolt of 1381

Following the death of Edward III in 1377, and during the minority of Richard II, the government of England suffered from a lack of leadership as troublesome as that which had existed during the illness of the Black Prince and the last years of the old king. Opposition to the interim rule of John of Gaunt was formidable, and his role in the surrender of English holdings on the Continent did not enhance his popularity. Moreover, the action taken by the good parliament of 1376 was arbitrarily repealed by the duke's maneuvers in 1377—a very discouraging blow to reformers, and a sore point with Londoners, whose hatred of the duke soon reached the boiling point.

The introduction of the poll tax in 1377 was designed both to force revenue from a sullen population and to pour money into faltering and unpopular enterprises. The resulting alienation of government and people was not unlike that experienced in modern times by the United States during the war in Vietnam. When the hated poll tax was renewed in 1379 and again in 1381, the tide of resentment could no longer be contained. In the month of May in Essex the first sporadic resistance to the tax appeared, followed by riots in Kent, which soon became the focal point of discontent. When the rebels occupied Maidstone, they freed from prison the radical priest, John Ball, whose sermons provided ideological substance to the movement, and they chose as their military leader Wat Tyler, who seems to have been in charge by the time they entered Canterbury without opposition on June 10, 1381. When the young King Richard sent word to the rebels, asking for an explanation, they replied that they wanted "to save him from his treacherous advisers."

On June 12 the rebels assembled outside London at Blackheath, and were joined by a group marching from Essex. It was here that John Ball preached his fiery sermon on the text "When Adam delved. . . ." The following day they crossed the Thames via London Bridge, and joined with the poor of the city in the destruction of the Savoy, John of Gaunt's palace on the Strand. The duke was in Scotland, else he might have perished in the flames or at the hands of the rebels. While the Savoy was burning, other bands were searching the city for "enemies," who mainly consisted of lawyers and other functionaries associated with the judicial system. Those they found were killed on the spot, usually by beheading.

On Friday, June 14, the king was at last able to arrange a meeting with the rebels at Mile End, but while these negotiations were in progress, others of the mob entered the Tower and seized several government leaders hiding there, the most prominent of whom was the chancellor, Simon Sudbury, archbishop of Canterbury. According to Walsingham, it took eight strokes of the amateur assassin's sword to decapitate the archbishop. His body lay unburied on the ground, while his head was stuck on a pole, paraded through the city, and then placed above the gate of London Bridge.

A final attempt to negotiate with the rebel leadership occurred on Saturday, June 15, at Smithfield. At this face-to-face meeting between Wat Tyler and the boy king, the fate of a nation hung in the balance. A frustrated group of leaders, including William of Walworth, mayor of London, had to watch while Tyler stood insolently before the king, making his demands, and menacingly tossing a dagger from hand to hand. At this moment, it seems, an argument broke out, during which the mayor knocked the peasant leader to the ground. This seemed to waken the king's men, who immediately pounced on Tyler and killed him. Seeing this, the rebels lost courage, and when Richard dramatically called upon them to accept his leadership, their forces dispersed and the rebellion soon came to an end.

Considering that royal promises of amnesty had been given under duress, the king and his advisers lost no time in seeking out and executing the leaders of the revolt and reestablishing control over the population. This reaction was in some ways severe, and in other ways merciful: many were executed, but many were forgiven. There also was, inevitably, an effort to identify and deal with the sources of the trouble. John Ball was drawn and quartered, but determined men like William Courtenay, who replaced Sudbury as archbishop of Canterbury, were convinced that Ball was merely a John the Baptist, and that the real heart of the rebelliousness could be located in the radical teachings of John Wyclif, Oxford scholar and reformer, who thus far had escaped censure by the Church because of his association with John of Gaunt. When the council at Blackfriars met in May of 1382 under Courtenay's leadership, it condemned certain of Wyclif's teachings, although it refrained from mentioning the reformer by name. Wyclif had already retired from Oxford to Lutterworth, and so the action at Blackfriars was employed as an instrument for the "purification" of Oxford University, which took place during the summer of 1382, and was completed by Courtenay himself during a convocation at Oxford in November of that year. Thereafter the Lollard movement, with which Wyclif was associated, continued without benefit of intellectual leadership in Oxford.

Historians of the Peasants' Revolt have found it difficult to define precisely the relationship between that event and the poem *Piers Plowman*. That there *is* a connection, of course, cannot be disputed. Correspondence between John Ball and some of his followers was recovered and preserved by some of the chroniclers, showing that the mad priest was not unfamiliar with the poem, as in this letter quoted by Walsingham (Dobson, 381):

> John Sheep, sometime Saint Mary's priest of York, and now of Colchester, greeteth well John Nameless, and John the Miller, and John Carter, and biddeth them that they beware of Guile in borough [A II 173–76], and standeth together in God's name, and biddeth Piers Plowman go to his work, and chastise well Hobbe the Robber [A V 233–50], and take with you John Trueman, and all his fellows, and no more, and look shape you to one head, and no more [i.e., agree on a single leader].
>
> John the Miller hath ground small, small, small. The King's son of heaven shall pay for all. Beware ere you be woe. Know your friend from your foe. Have enough and say "Whoa!" And do well and better [A *Vita*] and flee sin, and seek peace, and hold you therein. And so biddeth John Trueman and all his fellows.

Knighton preserves letters containing further allusions (Dobson, 381–83). Thus Jack Carter prays "that ye make a good end of that ye have begun, and do well and aye better and better. . . . Let Piers the Plowman my brother dwell at home and dight us corn [A VIII 5], and I will go with you and help that I may to dight your meat and drink, that ye none fail; look that Hobbe the Robber be well chastised for losing of your grace, for you have great need to take God with you in all your deeds. For now is time to beware." Here Robert the robber is invoked to reinforce the ban on looting, which as we have seen was ruthlessly enforced in the destruction of the Savoy.

Jack Trueman sends a message without verbal echoes of the poem, but with an emphasis that could well be indebted to it (Dobson, 382): "Jack Trueman doth you to understand that Falseness and Guile have reigned too long, and Truth hath been set under a lock, and Falseness reigneth in every flock. No man may come to Truth but he sing *si dedero*. Speak, spend, and speed, quoth John of Bathon, and therefore sin fareth as a wild flood, true love is away, that was so good, and clerks for wealth work them woe. God do best, for now is time." John Ball himself urges all manner of man (Dobson, 383) "to stand manly together in Truth, and help Truth, and Truth shall help you." And he concludes: "Now reigneth Pride in price [reputation], and Covetousness is held wise, and Lechery without shame, and Gluttony without blame. Envy reigns with Treason, and Sloth is taken in great season. God do boot, for now is time amen." It is interesting that Ball mentions precisely the six sins of the A version (V 45–259), omitting Wrath. Significantly, there are no verbal echoes in these letters that can be identified with anything peculiar to the B or C version.

Another contemporary witness, the writer responsible for that portion of the *Dieulacres Chronicle* covering the reign of Richard II, makes a curious mistake when he tells us that the peasants chose certain leaders among whom were "the abominable priest Johannes B [John Ball], Jack Straw, Piers Plowman and others bent on destroying the laws and customs of the kingdom. . . ." (Gray's Inn MS. no. 9, fol. 143r). Although the parallel is inexact, one is reminded of a similar error by the Roman historian Suetonius, who blames Claudius's expulsion of the Jews from Rome (ca. A.D. 52) on disturbances in the Jewish community created by one *Chrestus* (*Vita Claudi*, xxv.4; cf. Acts 18:2), over two decades after the Crucifixion.

Historians would have much less trouble understanding how *Piers Plowman* connects with the rising of 1381 if they had not been led by literary critics to view the poem as a single work by one author expressing one point of view. In fact, the peasants were inspired by the poem we know as the A version, and they knew nothing of its existence in any other form. Recent dialect studies by M. L. Samuels reveal that surviving manuscripts of A show a wide dialect distribution, while B and C manuscripts were mainly copied in a much more restricted area of the country from roughly Oxfordshire to the Severn estuary and Malvern hills. The first version reached a broad, popular audience; the B and C versions attracted a much more narrow (and intellectual) readership. Most important (to borrow a sentence from the description of the *Dieulacres Chronicle* by Clarke and Galbraith), *Piers Plowman* "turns out to be the composite product of two writers of strongly opposed views" (p. 125).

The emphasis on A in this Introduction truly reflects the impact of *Piers Plowman* during the lifetime of its authors. It is the A text that made the headlines, the A text that expresses the ideology that provided the foundation for the revolt. Was its author then a heretic, a revolutionary? Not at all. As Father Dunning's study proves, his teaching is quite orthodox. The incendiary ingredient of the A version is its sense of outrage at injustice, a feature that reminds us of the prophecies of Amos in the Old Testament. The prophet's anger over injustice led him to condemn those very features of Israel's religion that many of his contemporaries would have passionately defended. In *Piers Plowman* the emotion of our anonymous A poet communicated itself effectively to men who shared his outrage at injustice but who had their own ideas on what to do about it. Unfortunately Holy Church's reminder that love is the dearest thing (A I 178) was drowned in the roar of the peasant army that stormed over London Bridge in 1381.

Sister Francis Covella completed her dissertation at New York University in 1972 under the direction of Professor Lillian H. Hornstein. Its subject was "Formulaic Second Half-Lines in Skeat's A-text of *Piers Plowman*: Norms for a Comparative Analysis of the A-, B-, and C-texts." The experience of doing this close study of the metrical system of the A version, combined with a natural poetic gift, make Sister Francis an ideal translator of the poem. Although I have made some changes (mainly to do with uncertainties in the reading of the original text), I have found her talents ideally suited to the rendering of the alliterative long line into modern English. This line has four main stresses, with a variable number of unstressed syllables, forming a basic metrical pattern that looks like this:

> Me befel a ferly, of fairie me thoughte. (A Prologue 6)

The presence of a pause (caesura) between the first and second half of the line (after "ferly" here) led Skeat to separate the two half-lines thus:

> Me befel a ferly   of fairie me thoughte.

But this practice has been discontinued in modern editions of the poem, and so I have done likewise by treating the alliterative line as a single, four-stress unit in this translation. But Sister Francis, whose translation you are about to read, must have the last word:

> I have chosen to approximate this line in order to retain, as much as possible, the music of the A-version. The poet himself frequently deviates from this pattern in allowing the alliteration to fall on unaccented syllables, and in adding such syllables to the beginning of a half-line. In this translation, fidelity to the original sense and tone of the poem has had priority over sound patterns, but the general effect is, I hope, an echo of the original.

David C. Fowler
University of Washington

Background Reading

For a fuller discussion of *Piers Plowman*, including the B revision, see David C. Fowler, *The Bible in Middle English Literature*, Seattle: Univ. of Washington Press, 1984, chap. five, "Piers the Plowman as History," pp. 226–96, 304–14. Portions of this chapter relating to the A Version were adapted for use here in the Introduction. A valuable new bibliography has appeared: Derek Pearsall, *An Annotated Critical Bibliography of Langland*, Ann Arbor: the Univ. of Michigan Press, 1990. References given below are useful for study of the A Version or for historical background treated in the Introduction or Notes. Most modern scholarship on *Piers Plowman* is devoted exclusively to the B or C versions and is not included here. Of the following titles, Father Dunning's book is particularly recommended.*

Alford, John A., ed. *A Companion to Piers Plowman*. Berkeley: Univ. of California Press, 1988.

Alford, John A. *Piers Plowman: A Guide to the Quotations*. Binghamton: Medieval and Renaissance Texts and Studies, 1992.

Bennett, Josephine Waters. "The Mediaeval Loveday," *Speculum* 33 (1958): 351–70.

Clarke, M. V. and V. H. Galbraith. "The Deposition of Richard II," *John Rylands Library Bulletin* 14 (1930): 164–81.

Dobson, R. B. *The Peasants' Revolt of 1381*. London: Macmillan, 1970.

*Dunning, Thomas P. *Piers Plowman: An Interpretation of the A Text*. Dublin: The Talbot Press, Ltd., 1937 (2nd ed., rev. and ed. T. P. Dolan. Oxford: Clarendon Press, 1980).

Hilton, Rodney H. *Bond Men Made Free: Medieval Peasant Movements and the English Rising of 1381*. London: Temple Smith, 1973.

Kirk, Elizabeth D. *The Dream Thought of Piers Plowman*. New Haven and London: Yale Univ. Press, 1972.

Owst, G. R. *Preaching in Medieval England*. Cambridge: Cambridge Univ. Press, 1926.

Owst, G. R. *Literature and Pulpit in Medieval England*. Cambridge: Cambridge Univ. Press, 1933 (2nd ed., rev., Oxford: Basil Blackwell, 1961).

Pantin, W. A. *The English Church in the Fourteenth Century*. Cambridge: Cambridge Univ. Press, 1955.

Revard, Carter. "*Title* and *Auaunced* in *Piers Plowman* B.11.290," *Yearbook of Langland Studies* I (1987): 116–21.

Walsh, Katherine. *A Fourteenth Century Scholar and Primate: Richard FitzRalph in Oxford, Avignon and Armagh*. Oxford: Clarendon Press, 1981.

Editions consulted:

Skeat, Walter W. *Piers the Plowman in Three Parallel Texts*. 2 vols. Oxford: Clarendon Press, 1886.

Knott, Thomas A. and David C. Fowler. *Piers the Plowman: A Critical Edition of the A-Version*, Baltimore: The Johns Hopkins Press, 1952.

Kane, George. *Piers Plowman: The A-Version*. London: The Athlone Press, 1960 (Rev. ed., Univ. of California Press, 1988).

Note: Latin quotations are identified in the footnotes, and translations provided when the poet does not give one, or translates freely. The Douay Bible is used for translations of scripture, since it is closest to the Latin Vulgate (=V) employed by the author.

Prologue

One season in summer when the sun's rays were soft,
I clad myself in clothing as coarse as a shepherd's
In the habit of a hermit unholy in works
I wandered far in this world wonders to hear.
There befell me a marvel, pure magic it seemed.
A strange event befell me; a fantasy, I thought.
I was weary of wandering and went aside to rest
Under a broad bank by a brook's side.
And as I lay languidly and looked at the water
I soon fell asleep, it sounded so merry.
    Then did I dream a marvelous dream,
That I was in a wilderness; I did not know where.
And as I looked toward the east in the light of the sun,
I saw a tower on a hill artfully made.
Beneath was a deep dale a dungeon within
With a ditch deep and dark and dreadful to see.[1]
A fair field full of folk I found there between
Of all kinds of people, the poor and the rich,
Working and wandering as the world requires.
    Some became plowmen and played very seldom;
In planting and sowing they struggled quite hard,
Produced what the shiftless with gluttony destroyed.
And some practiced pride, pompously dressed;
Under cover of clothing were cunningly disguised.
In prayer and in penance others pledged to remain;
For love of our Lord lived ascetical lives,

---

[1] The "dungeon" (in Middle English) is a "keep," a central tower in the defence system of the medieval castle, here located in a dark valley and surrounded by a moat.

In the hope they would have heavenly bliss.
As anchorites and hermits who held to their cells,
They cared not to canter in the country about,
Looking for a life of luxury and ease.
And some chose to bargain the better to prosper,
As it seems, to our thinking, that such men thrive.
And some chose to make merry as minstrels can do,
And get gold with their glee, guiltless, I believe.
But tale-tellers and jesters, Judas' children
Fashion false fantasies and make themselves fools,
And yet have wit at their will to work if they pleased.
What Paul preaches against them I dare not prove here,[1]
Whoever speaks scandal is Lucifer's slave.
Bidders and beggars went quickly about
Till their bags and their bellies were filled to the brim;
They feigned need for their food, fought at the alehouse,
In gluttony, God knows, they go to their beds,
And rise up with ribaldry as Robert's bold knaves;
Sleep and slothfulness pursue them forever.
Pilgrims and palmers promised each other
To seek the shrine of Saint James and saints at Rome;
They went forth on their way with many wise tales,
And had leave to lie all their lives after.
Hordes of hermits, with their hooked staves,
Went off to Walsingham; their wenches followed after.
Big muscular fellows who cared not for work
Clothed themselves in copes to capture attention;
Dressed themselves as hermits to have a life of ease.
I found there friars, all the four orders,
Preaching to the people to profit themselves;
Glossing the gospel as seemed good to them
Covetous of clothing, construed it as they pleased.
Many of these masters may dress as they like,
For money and merchandise meet often together.[2]
Since Charity has turned trader, and traffics in confessions,
Many wonders have happened in a few years.
Unless Holy Church and the orders cherish each other,
The greatest mischief on earth is mounting up fast.[3]

[1] A few MSS cite 2 Thess. 3:10; the source of 39a is unknown.

[2] Cf. Chaucer, *Canterbury Tales* A319: "Of fees and robes hadde he many oon."

[3] Probably refers to the conflict between Archbishop Richard FitzRalph and the friars in London, 1356–57. See Dunning (1937, p. 20; 1980, p. 9) and Walsh (1981, pp. 406–21).

A pardoner preached there as if he were priest;
Presented a scroll with seals of the bishop
And said he himself could absolve them all there
Of feigning to fast and of holy vows broken.
The unlearned liked him and believed what he said,
Came up on their knees and kissed the decree.
He poked at them with his brevet[1] and bleared their eyes,
And raked in with this ragman rings and brooches.
Thus you give of your gold to help greedy gluttons,
And leave it to lechers who practice foul lust.
Were the bishop truly blessed and worth both his ears,
He would not send his seal to deceive the people.
Yet blame not the bishop for all the knave's preaching.
The parish priest and pardoner share in the profit
That the poor people of the parish should have.
Parsons and parish priests complained to their bishop
That their parishes have been poor since pestilence time;
And asked license and leave at London to dwell,
To sing there for simony for silver is sweet.
There hovered a hundred in hoods of pure silk,
Sergeants, it seemed, who served at the bar,
Pleaded for profit and expounded the law;
Not for love of our Lord would they open their lips.
You might better mete the mist on Malvern's high hills,
Than get a mumble from their mouth until money was showed.
I saw bishops bold and bachelors of divinity
Become clerks of accounts in service to the king.
Archdeacons and deans who have the great duty
To preach to the people, provide food for the poor,
Have run down to London by leave of their bishops
To be clerks of the king's bench the country to ruin.
Barons and burgesses and bondmen as well
I saw in that assembly, as you shall hear shortly;
Bakers and butchers and brewers aplenty;
Woolweavers there were and weavers of linen;
Tailors and tanners, and treaters of wool,
Masons and miners, and many other craftsmen;
Ditchers and diggers who do their work badly,
And while away the day with "God save you, Dame Emme."
Cooks and their helpers cry "Hot pies, hot!

[1] The brevet was the pardoner's letter of indulgence, an authorization which he carried, probably in the form of a scroll. It is also referred to pejoratively as a "ragman" (72).

Good geese and fat pigs; let us go dine."
Taverners told them the very same tale:
"Good wine of Gascony and wine of Alsace,
Of Rhine and of Rochelle go well with a roast!"
All this I saw sleeping and seven times more.

PASSUS I

The meaning of this mountain and the dark, murky dale,
And this field full of folk, I will faithfully show.
A lady, lovely of face, and clothed in white linen
Came down from the cliff, and kindly she called me
And said, "Son, are you sleeping? Do you see all these people
How busy they are, bustling about?
Most of the people who pass through this world,
Have they honor on this earth, they aspire to no better.
Of other heaven than here, they have no regard."
In awe of her face although she was fair,
I said, "Mercy, my Lady, what does this mean?"
"In the tower on the hill," said she, "Truth may be found,
And would that you worked as His word teaches;
For He is father of faith who fashioned you all,
Your face and your features, and gave you five wits
To worship Him with while you are here.
He commanded the earth to help you each one
With wool and with linen, and food needful for life,
In moderate manner to make you at ease.
And commanded of His courtesy in common three things,
None as needful as these, so name them I will,
By rule and by reason; repeat them hereafter.
One is clothing to shield you from cold;
And another is food to fend off disease;
And drink when you're dry, but don't overdo it.
You'll be worse if you do when you should be working.
For Lot in his life-time addicted to liquor
Did with his daughters what the devil approved;
Delighted in drink as the devil would have it.
This led to lechery and he lay by them both.
He blamed all on wine for that wicked deed.[1]
Dread drinking for pleasure and you shall do better;

[1] Gen. 19:30–38.

Measure is medicine, though you yearn for more.
All is not good for the spirit what the senses demand,
Nor support for the body what pleases the soul.
Believe not your body, for a liar is its teacher;
That is the wicked world which would betray you.
The fiend and your flesh follow together,
Corrupting your soul; keep this in mind.
And because you should beware, a better way I teach you."
"Ah, Madame, thank you!" said I, "your words I like well,
But the money in this world that men value so much,
Tell me, to whom does that treasure belong?"
"Go to the gospel," said she, "where Christ Himself speaks.[1]
When people in the temple presented Him a penny,
And inquired should they honor with it Caesar as king,
He asked them to whom the inscription referred,
And whose image it was impressed on its side.
'Caesar,' they said, 'we see that quite well.'
'Then *render to Caesar*,' said Christ, 'what *to Caesar* belongs,
And to God what is God's, or else you transgress.'
For rightfully Reason should rule over all,
And Common Sense be warden your wealth to preserve,
And guardian of your treasure to give you at need;
For economy and good sense go well together."
Then I questioned her meekly by Him who made her:
"The dungeon in the dale that is dreadful to see,
What may it mean? Madam, I ask you."
"That is the Castle of Care," said she; "whoever comes in this place,
May bewail that he was born in body or soul.
There dwells a wretch, Wrong is he called,
Father of falseness, he founded it himself.
Adam and Eve he incited to sin,
Counselled bold Cain to kill his own brother.
He also tricked Judas with the Jews' silver,
Who on an elder tree hanged himself after.
Wrong is enemy to love and to everyone lies.
Those who trust in his treasure are quickly betrayed."
Then I wondered in my mind what woman it was,
Who with words of such wisdom Holy Writ showed me,
And besought her in God's name before she went away
Who she was, truly, who taught me so well.
"Holy Church," said she; "surely you know me.
It was I first received you and taught you your faith.

[1] Matt. 22:17–21.

You brought me pledges my bidding to do,
And to love me loyally while your life lasts."
Then quickly I kneeled and cried her for grace,
And pleaded with her earnestly to pray for my sins,
And to teach me truly in Christ to believe,
And to accomplish His will who created me man.
"Teach me of no treasure but tell me one thing:
How I may save my soul, you who are saintly."
"When all treasures are tried truth is the best.
I appeal to *Deus caritas* to deem the truth.[1]
It is as precious a love token as dear God Himself.
Whoever is true of tongue, tells nothing else,
Works by that teaching and wills no man harm,
He is a god, says the gospel, both here and hereafter,
And is likened to our Lord in Saint Luke's words.[2]
The learned who know this should announce it to all,
For both Christian and heathen lay claim to the truth.
Kings and their knights should have it in care,
And make haste to ride in the realms all about,
Taking trespassers of the law and tying them up,
Till Truth has determined their trespass and doom.
For David, in his time, dubbed many knights,
Made them swear on their sword to serve truth forever.
That is the profession proper to knights,
Not to fast one Friday in five score years,
But side with him and with her who strive for justice,
And never leave them for love or unlawful gifts.
He who forgets that plain fact is faithless to his order.
For Christ, King of kings, created ten choirs,
Cherubim and seraphim and seven orders plus one,
Gave them power of His majesty, which pleased them the more,
And over His kingdom crowned them archangels,
And taught through the Trinity understanding of truth.
To obey His commands, that was all He required.
"Lucifer with his legions learned this in heaven.
He was the loveliest to look on after our Lord,
Till he broke that commandment because of his pride.
Then he fell with his followers and fiends they became;
Out of heaven to hell helter-skelter they fled:
Some in air, some on earth and some in deep hell.
But Lucifer lay the lowest of all;

[1] 1 John 4:6–8, "God is love."
[2] John 10:34 (alluding to Ps. 82:6); cf. Luke 6:35.

For yielding to pride his pain has no end.
All who work with the devil shall depart the same way
On the day of their death and dwell with that shrew.
But they who work by the word that Holy Writ teaches,
And end, as I've said, in perfect works,
May be sure that their souls shall ascend into heaven
Where Truth is in Trinity and receives them in triumph.
"So I say, as I said, and the Scriptures affirm it:[1]
When all treasures are tried, Truth is the best.
Teach this to laymen, for the learned know it,
That Truth is the choicest treasure on earth."
"I have no innate knowledge," said I, "so you must teach me
Where in my body this knowledge begins."
"You dumb dolt," said she, "your wits are quite dull.
Inborn understanding instructs you in the heart
To love your Lord better than you love yourself
And to avoid deadly sin though you should die.
I trust this is truth; whoever can teach better
Allow him to speak; then instruct others after.
For thus His word teaches: your works should be witness
That love is the dearest thing our Lord asks of us,
And also the plant of peace; preach this on your harp
When merry at meals and men bid you to sing.
For your heart's understanding gives rise to a power
That comes from the Father who fashioned us all;
He looked on us lovingly and let His son die,
Who meekly for misdeeds made amends for us all.
Yet He willed not to punish those who caused Him that pain,
But meekly He murmured, and mercy He sought,
Had pity on that people who put Him to death.
"You may see here an example in His own life:
He was mighty yet meek and mercy could grant
To those who hung Him on high, and pierced his heart.
So I counsel the rich: remember the poor.
Though you be mighty in court, be meek in your deeds;
For with the measure you use, whether wrong or right,
You shall be judged yourself when your journey is ended.[2]
For though truthful in word and honest in work,
And as chaste as a child weeping in Church,
Unless you love truly and tend to the poor,
Of such goods as God sends you share with them all,

[1] Matt. 22:17–21 and 1 John 4:6–8.
[2] Matt. 7:2, James 2:13.

You will have no more merit in Mass nor in Matins
Than Malkyn of her maidenhood that no man desires.
For Saint James the Apostle proclaimed in his book
That faith without works is worth nothing at all
And dead as a doornail unless the deed follow.
Chastity without charity shall be chained in hell,
Useless as a lamp without a light in it.
"Many chaplains are chaste but charity is absent;
None more heartless than they, when they are beneficed.[1]
Unkind to their kin and to all fellow Christians,
They chew up their charity, then chide after more.
Such chastity without charity shall be chained in hell.
You curates who keep yourselves clean only in body
Are encumbered with greed and cannot creep out,
So hard has avarice hasped you together.[2]
That is not the truth of Trinity but the treachery of hell,
And a lesson for the laity to delay giving alms.
"For these are God's words written in the gospel:
Give and it shall be given you[3] for I give to you all.
That is the latch of love that lets out My grace
To comfort the sorrowful encumbered with sin.
Love is the dearest thing our Lord asks of us,
And also the highway that leads into heaven.
So I repeat what I said, by sight of these texts:
When all treasures are tried, truth is the best.
Now have I told you what truth is that no treasure is better,
I may linger no longer; may our Lord preserve you."

PASSUS II

Still kneeling before her a favor I asked,
And said, "Please, my lady, for love of heaven's queen
Who bore the blessed babe that bought our salvation,
Teach me the skill to discern what is false."
"Look on the left," said she, "and lo, there he stands,
Both Falsehood and Flattery and all their false friends."

---

[1] "beneficed": see Revard (1987). A "benefice is an ecclesiastical office, or the income derived from it."

[2] Covetous curates are locked inside their own money boxes; only the "latch of love" (177) offers hope of escape from their self-imposed prison.

[3] Luke 6:38.

I looked on the left side as the lady instructed,
And was aware of a woman wonderfully clothed,
Her robe edged with fur, the richest on earth,
Crowned with a crown, the king has none better.
All her five fingers were fretted with rings
Of the most precious stones that prince ever wore.
Robed in red scarlet and ribboned with gold,
There lives no lady more lovely than she.[1]
"Who is this woman," said I, "so wonderfully attired?"
"Meed the maiden," said she, "much mischief she's done me;
Belittled my teaching to lords all about.
In the pope's palace, she's as privy as myself;
And that should not be since Wrong was her sire.
She was fostered by Wrong, wrought misfortune to many.
I should be above her, for my lineage is better.
"Tomorrow will be the marriage of Meed and of False;
Flattery with fair speech has forged them together,
Guile has besieged her so, she grants what he wills;
And it is Liar who leads them to lie together.
"Tomorrow False will marry Lady Meed, as I've said.
There witness if you will who they all are
Who belong to that lordship, the less and the more.
Know them there if you can and keep from them all,
If you want to abide with Truth in his bliss.
I may no longer delay: to our Lord I commend you,
Become a good man, and avoid greed, I advise."
All the rich retinue that reigned there with False,
Were invited to the bridal; from all sides they came.
Sir Simony is sent for, to put his seal on the charters
That False and Flattery had any fair claim to,
And with them grant Meed in marriage forever.
No hall nor house could harbor the people:
Every field was full of folk all about.
In the midst of a mountain, at midmorning time
Was pitched a pavilion proud for the occasion,
And ten thousand tents were set up beside
For knights of the country and newcomers about,
For jurors, for summoners, for sellers, for buyers,
For lay folk, for learned, for laborers of towns,

[1] The original is difficult to translate: "There is no quen queyntere that quyk is o lyue." Both "quen" and "queyntere" are susceptible to secondary ironic interpretation that undercuts the apparent praise of Lady Meed. (Compare Shakespeare's use of "queen" and "quean".)

All there to witness what the writ would contain,
What Meed was granted as gifts for her marriage;
To fasten her to False, the fee was arranged.
Then Flattery fetches her and gives her to False
On condition that Falsehood will provide for her always,
And she be humble and docile and do what he asks,
In bed and at board be obedient and polite,
And as Sir Simony will say, serve at his will.
Simony and Civil stand before all
Unfolding the deed that Falseness had made,
And thus began this pair and proclaimed in loud voice:
"Know this and witness it, ye that dwell upon earth,
That I, Flattery, grant to Falsehood the fair maiden Meed,
To be present in pride for poor or for rich
With the earldom of envy forever to last,
With all the lordship of lechery in length and in breadth,
With the kingdom of covetousness I crown them together,
And all the isle of usury and the stronghold of avarice.
Gluttony and great oaths I give them together
With all delights of lust the devil to serve;
In the seigniory of sloth I seize them together
To have and to hold and all their heirs after,
With all the appurtenance of purgatory into punishment in hell,
Yielding for this union at one year's end
Their souls to Satan who will sink them in pain,
To dwell there with Wrong while God is in heaven."
To witness this writ Wrong was the first,
Then Piers, the pardoner, a doctor of the Paulines,
Bart the beadle, of Buckinghamshire,
Randolf the reeve, in the district of Rutland,
Munde the miller, and many such rogues.
In the date of the devil the deed was sealed,
In the sight of Sir Simony and signed by the notaries.
Then Theology was vexed when he heard this news,
And said then to Civil, "Now sorrow on your books
Such a wedding to witness which will anger Truth;
If this wedding is sealed, may sorrow befall you!
For Meed is an honest woman, born of Amends;
God granted that Meed be given to Truth,
But you gave her to a liar. May God give you sorrow!
That is not Scripture's teaching; Truth knows the truth:
'Worthy is the workman to have his reward,'[1]

[1] Matt. 10:10.

But you have enfeoffed her to False. Fie on your law!
For you live all by lies and lecherous affairs;
You and Sir Simony shame Holy Church.
You and the notaries annoy the poor people.
You shall pay for it, both of you, by the God who made me!
For you know well, you liars, unless your wit fail,
That False is a phony, a do-nothing fake;
A bastard from birth, Beelzebub's kin.
And Meed is a woman, a maiden of worth.
She might kiss the king as cousin if she wished.
Act wisely if you will with understanding as well;
Lead her to London where law is decided,
Whether it's legal to allow them to lie together.
And if the justice will judge her to be joined with False,
Yet beware of the wedding; much wiser is Truth.
For Conscience is of his counsel and knows you quite well.
If he finds you at fault for siding with False,
Your souls shall be punished with pain at the end."
    Civil gave his assent but Simony would not
Till he had silver for his seals and signs.
Then Flattery brought forth florins enough
And bade Guile go to work and give gold all about,
To the notaries, namely, that their needs be met:
"And bribe False-witness with florins enough
For he can master Lady Meed and mold her to my will."
When this gold was given great were the thanks
To False and to Flattery for their fair gifts.
And they came to comfort False for his cares
And swore to him, "Certainly we'll never cease
Till Meed be your wedded wife; we'll see to that.
We have so mastered Meed with many fine words
That she agrees to go with a good will
To inquire in London if the law would
Judge you to be jointly in joy forever."
    Then was False pleased and Flattery blithe,
Summoning all men from the shires about,
And all to be bound, beggars and others,
To go with them to Westminster to witness this deed.
Then they clamored for horses to carry them there,
And Flattery brought forth the finest of foals,
And set Meed on a sheriff, shod all new,
And False on a juror's back jogged gently along,
And Flattery sat on Fair Speech, finely attired.
    The notaries had no horses and were greatly annoyed
That Simony and Civil should travel on foot.

Then Civil was resentful, and swore by the cross,
That summoners should be saddled and serve everyone.
"Let Provisors be apparelled as palfreys or ponies;
Sir Simony himself shall sit on their backs.
And let all deans and subdeans be dressed as great chargers,
For they shall bear bishops and bring them to rest.
People of the Paulines for their complaints in consistory
Shall serve only myself; Civil am I called.
Let our commissary be harnessed, our cart he shall draw,
And fetch all our foodstuffs from dealers in lust.
And make Liar a long cart to lead all the others,
Tramps and tale-tellers that tittup on foot."
Now False and Flattery come forth together
With Meed in the middle and more in their train.
I have no leisure to tell of the trail that followed,
Of all kinds of people who populate this earth,
But Guile was in front and guided them all.
Truthfulness saw them and said very little,
But spurred on his palfrey and soon passed them all,
Came to the king's court and reported to Conscience.
Conscience went to the king and recounted the message.
"Now by Christ," said the king, "could I but catch
False or Flattery or any of their followers,
I would wreak vengeance on these wretches who do so much harm,
Hang them up by the neck, and all who support them.
No one in the world shall go bail for the least:
Whatever the law decides, let happen to all."
He commanded a constable who came in all haste:
"Arrest these tyrants, I tell you, and don't touch any bribes.
Fetter False fast; refuse all of his gifts.
And strike off Guile's head, let him go no farther;
And bring Meed to me in spite of them all.
To Simony and to Civil I send this stern warning:
Because of them Holy Church will be harmed forever.
And if you catch Liar, let him not escape
Being put on the pillory, however he plead."
Dread at the door stood and heard the king's doom,
And quickly he went to warn False and his friends.
And bade him flee for fear, and his followers also.
Then False, out of fear, flew to the friars,
And Guile got ready to go, aghast at his fate.
But merchants soon met him and made him abide,
Shut him up in their shops to show their wares,
Dressed him as an apprentice the people to serve.
Liar was light, and leapt nimbly away,

Lurking in lanes, dragged about by the ears.
Nowhere was he welcome when he told his false tales
But everywhere taunted and told to be gone,
Till pardoners had pity and pulled him inside,
Washed him and wiped him and wound him in rags,
And sent him on Sundays with false seals to Church
Where he gave pardon for pence pound at a time.
Physicians then frowned, and forwarded letters,
Asked him to reside with them and examine urine.
Grocers too spoke with him to inspect their goods,
For he knew well their craft and could name many spices.
Minstrels and messengers met with him once,
Detained him for half a year and eleven days more.
Fair speaking friars fetched him from there,
And to prevent recognition, dressed him as a friar;
But he has permission to leave whenever he likes,
And is welcome to return, and tarries with them often.
Thus all fled for fear and flew into corners;
Except Meed the maiden, no more dared to stay,
But truly to tell she trembled for fear,
And wrung her hands weeping when she was arrested.

PASSUS III

Now Meed the maid, and no more of that crowd,
With beadles and bailiffs is brought to the king.
Then the king called a clerk (I recall not his name)
To take Meed the maiden, and make her feel at ease:
"I shall examine her myself and ask her, in truth,
What man in this world is dearest to her;
If she take my advice and obey my commands,
I shall forgive her this guilt, so help me God."
Courteously the clerk then, as the king commanded,
Took Meed by the middle and brought her to chamber.
There was much mirth and music to please Lady Meed:
Those residing at Westminster all worship her there.
Gently, with joy, the Justices gathered,
Bustled to the bower where the bride was,
Comforted her kindly by clergy's leave,
And said, "Mourn not Lady Meed nor make yourself sad.
We will instruct the king and smooth well your way,
For all that Conscience's craft and contrivance can do."
Graciously then Meed gave thanks to them all

For their great goodness, and gave everyone
Bowls of pure gold and pieces of silver,
Rings with bright rubies and riches abundant;
The least of that crowd received a gold coin.
Then bowing to that lady, these lords took their leave.
Then came the clerks to comfort her too,
And bade her be blithe, "for we are your men,
To do what you will while our lives last."
Sweetly she smiled then and promised the same:
To love them loyally and make them all lords,
And in consistory at court to call out their names.
"No ignorance shall hinder him that I love
From being first advanced, for I am well known,
While clerks who are learned shall go limping behind."
Then came a confessor in the cope of a friar.
To Meed the maiden meekly he bowed,
And said very softly, in shrift, as it were:
"Though learned and unlearned had lain by your side,
And though False had followed you for fifteen long years,
I shall absolve you myself, for a small share of wheat,
And be also your bawd and do what you bid
Among clerks and knights, causing conscience to fail."
Then Meed for her misdeeds kneeled to that man
And confessed all her sins, shameless, I think.
She told him a tale and tossed him a coin
To make him her beadsman and her bawd also.
He absolved her sins quickly, and then he said,
"We are working on a window which will cost a great deal;
If you furnish the glass and engrave your name there,
Your soul shall be sure of a heavenly home."
"Were that so," said the woman, "no window nor altar
Should I not make or mend and mark my name there,
So that all seeing would say I am a sister of your house."
But God forbids such engraving to every good person:
"Let not your left hand neither early nor late
Be aware what your right hand is working or doing."[1]
But do your giving in private so that pride has no part,
Neither outwardly nor inwardly, for God is aware
Who is courteous or kind, covetous or otherwise.
Thus I admonish you, lords, to avoid these engravings,
Such as writing in windows of your good works
Or proclaiming to the people when you give to the poor,

[1] Matt. 6:3.

Lest perchance you receive your reward here on earth.
For our Savior has said this and preached it Himself:[1]
Amen I say to you, they have received their reward.
Mayors and magistrates are meant to be mediators
Between the king and the commons, to keep the laws well
By punishing in pillories or on public stools
Brewers and bakers, butchers and cooks,
Who are men of the world that do the most harm
To the poor people who purchase piece-meal.
They poison the people privily and often,
And get rich through retailing and the buying of rentals
With what the poor people should put in their mouths.
Had they given good measure, they would not build so high
Nor have such fine tenements, be certain of that!
But Meed the maiden pleaded with the mayor
To accept silver coins from all such tradesmen,
Or presents not in currency, such as cups of silver,
Rings or other riches, retailers to maintain.
"For my love," said the lady, "love them each one,
And suffer them to sell somewhat unreasonably."
But Solomon the sage once had a saying
To amend mayors and men who enforce the law;
And told them this theme that I'll tell to you:[2]
Ignis devorabit tabernacula eorum qui libenter accipiunt munera.
Among learned lords, these Latin words mean
That fire shall descend and destroy in the end
The houses and homes of those who desire
To accept gifts as bribes in youth or in age.
The king came from council and called for Lady Meed,
Sent a sergeant to fetch her as swiftly as he could,
And he brought her to bower with bliss and with joy.
Courteously the king then commences to speak,
To Meed the maiden addresses these words:
"Unwisely, woman, have you often acted;
But you never did worse, than when you took False.
Yet I forgive you this guilt and grant you my grace
If hence, to your dying day, you do so no more.
I have a knight named Conscience, just come from abroad,
If he take you for wife, will you accept him?"
"Yes, lord," said that lady, "the Lord forbid else!

[1] Matt. 6:2.

[2] Job 15:34. Job is part of the Old Testament wisdom literature, which was often attributed to Solomon (see line 81).

Unless I keep your command you can hang me at once."
Then Conscience was called for to come and appear
Before the king and his council, clerks and all others.
Kneeling there, Conscience bowed to the king,
To know what his will was, and what he should do.
"Will you wed this woman," said the king, "if I approve?
She is eager for your fellowship, to be your true mate."
"No," said Conscience then, "Christ forbid such a thing!
Before I wed such a wife woe come upon me!
She is frail of her faith and fickle of speech;
She makes men do evil many score times.
Trusting her treasure causes trouble to many;
To wives and to widows wantonness she teaches,
And they learn of lechery who love her fair gifts.
Your father she felled with her false promises,[1]
Poisoned some popes and impaired Holy Church.
There is no better bawd, by Him that made me,
Between heaven and hell though men searched the whole earth.
She has a ticklish tail and a tale-bearing tongue,
As common as the cart-way to all kinds of knaves:
To monks and to minstrels, to lepers in hedges.
Jurors and summoners, such men praise her;
Sheriffs of shires would be ruined without her.
She makes men lose their land and their lives also,
Lets prisoners loose and pays bribes for them often.
She gives gold to the jailor and great coins besides,
To unfetter false men, let them flee where they please.
She takes the true man by the top and ties him tight,
And hangs him out of hate though he never did harm.
If she is cursed in consistory, she could not care less,
For she gives copes to the commissary and coats to the clerks.
She is absolved just as soon as it pleases herself.
She may do nigh as much in one month alone,
As your secret seal may in seven score days.
She is privy with the pope; provisors know this.
Sir Simony and herself seal all the bulls;
She blesses the bishops though they be unlearned.
She gets prebends for parsons, and priests she supports
To keep paramours and lovers all the days of their lives,
And bring forth babies forbidden by law.
Where a king welcomes her, woe is that realm!
For she gives favors to False and befouls Truth often.

[1] A reference to the murder of Edward II in Berkeley Castle in 1327.

To barons and burgesses she brings great sorrow;
With her jewels, by Jesus, your judges she corrupts,
Unlawfully lies and obstructs the truth,
Until faith cannot go forward against the blizzard of her florins.
She conducts law as she pleases and love-days she makes,[1]
To the poor man's confusion though he plead forever.
Law is so lordly and reluctant to settle,
That without presents or pence she pleases very few.
Clergy and covetousness she couples together.
This the life of that lady. Our Lord give her sorrow!
And to all who maintain her may misfortune befall them!
For the poor have no power to protest though they suffer,
Such a master is Meed among men of wealth."
    Then Meed cried aloud and complained to the king
And asked leave to speak to succeed if she might.
The king granted that favor with a good will:
"Excuse yourself if you can; I can say no more now.
For Conscience accuses you to dismiss you forever."
"No, lord," said that lady, "never believe him,
When you know truly where the wrong lies.
Where mischief is great, Meed may provide help.
Of course you know, Conscience, I came not to chide
Nor to slander your person with a proud heart.
You are well aware, Conscience, unless you will lie,
You have hung on my neck a number of times;
And grasped at my gold and gave where you pleased.
It's a wonder, indeed, that you're so angry now!
Yet power do I have to honor you with gifts,
To maintain your manhood more than you know.
You have defamed me unfairly before the king here,
For I never killed a king or counselled it either,
Nor ever did as you deem, I leave it up to the king.
    "In Normandy he was not annoyed for my sake;
But you yourself, certainly, shamed him there often,[2]
Crept into a cabin to keep your nails warm,
Believed that long winter would have lasted forever,
And dreaded to die in a dark storm;
Then you hastened homeward because you were hungry.
Without pity, you pillager, poor men you robbed,

[1] For "love-days" see Bennett (1958). These were days set aside for the voluntary settlement of legal disputes by arbitration. See also XI 20, 209.

[2] References are to the Norman wars, especially the Treaty of Bretigny in 1360 (191–93). Efforts to date this passage a decade later are unconvincing.

And bore their brass on your back to barter in Calais.
But I stayed with my lord to save his life,
Made him merry as a means of mitigating grief,
Patted him on the back, emboldened his heart,
Made him dance at the thought that I was there when he wanted.
Had I been marshall of his men, by Mary in heaven,
I would have wagered my life and no less pledged
He'd be lord of that land in length and in breadth,
And also king of that country to help his own kin,
The least brat of his blood the peer of a baron.
But you coward, Conscience, you counselled his return
To leave that lordship for a little silver,
The richest of realms that rain falls upon!
"It is fitting for a king who governs a realm
To give meed to his followers who faithfully serve him;
To favor with gifts foreigners and others.
Meed makes him beloved and esteemed as a man.
Emperors and earls and lords of all kinds,
Through gifts, have retainers to run and to ride.
The pope and his prelates take presents at times
And reward men themselves to maintain their own laws.
Servants for their service (we see this truth well)
Take meed from their masters as they may agree.
Beggars for prayers beg men for meed;
Minstrels for merrymaking ask meed in return.
The king takes meed from his men to make peace in the land;
Those who teach clerks tuition require;
Priests who preach sermons instructing the people
Expect meed and mass-pence and their meals also.
All kinds of craftsmen crave meed for apprentices;
Meed and merchandizing must needs go together.
No one, I believe, may live without meed."
Then the king said to Conscience, "By Christ, it seems clear,
Meed must be worthy the mastery to have."
"No," Conscience cried, and kneeled to the king,
"There are two kinds of meed, my lord, by your leave:
One that God through His grace gives in His goodness,
To those who do well while they dwell here.
The prophet has preached this and put it in the psalter:[1]
Qui pecuniam suam non dedit ad usuram, etc.
Take no meed, my lord, from men who are true;

[1] Ps. 15:5. (V 14:5). "he that hath not put out his money to usury, nor taken bribes against the innocent."

Love them and lend to them for love of our Lord;
God's meed and His mercy then you may win.
But there is a meed without measure that magistrates desire;
To maintain miscreants this meed they demand.
Thereof speaks the psalter at the end of a psalm:[1]
In quorum manibus iniquitates sunt; dextera eorum repleta est muneribus.
And those that grasp such gifts, so help me God,
Shall pay for it bitterly, or the holy book lies!
Priests and parsons who desire vain pleasure,
And take meed and money for masses they sing,
Have their reward in this world, as Matthew has written:[2]
Amen, amen, receperunt mercedem suam.
That laborers and poor men take money from masters
Is no kind of meed, but a reasonable wage.
Nor is meed in commerce; with that I concur.
That is simply an exchange, one penny-worth for another.
"But did you never read in Kings, you recreant Meed,
Why vengeance fell suddenly on Saul and his children?
God sent a message by Samuel's mouth,
That Agag of Amalek and all of his people
Should die for a deed that their elders had done
Against Israel and Aaron and Moses his brother.
Samuel said to Saul: 'God sends this command:
Be obedient and bound to do his bidding.
Go with your cohorts and kill all the women,
Servants and children, chop them to death.
You must kill the king but covet not his goods,
Nor his millions in money; murder each one,
Children and beasts, burn all to ashes.'
Since he killed not the king as God had commanded,
And coveted his goods and killed not his beasts,
But brought them back with him as the bible recounts,
God said to Samuel that Saul had to die
And all his sons for that sin shamefully perish.
Such great misfortune Meed caused the king
That God hated him and all his heirs after.
The crux of this case I care not to show;
Lest perchance it annoy me, I'll come to an end.
I, Conscience, know this, for common sense taught me
That reason shall reign and govern many realms.

---

[1] Ps. 26:10 (V 25:10). "In whose hands are iniquities: their right hand is filled with gifts."

[2] Matt. 6:2. "Amen I say to you, they have received their reward."

What happened to Agag shall happen to others;
Samuel shall slay him and Saul shall be blamed,
David be crowned and conquer them all,
And one Christian King shall care for each one.
No longer shall Meed be master on earth,
But love and lowliness and loyalty together.
Whoever sins against Truth by taking a bribe,
Loyalty shall prosecute, or else lose his life.
No sergeant for that service shall wear a silk hood
Nor a striped robe, trimmed with rich fur.
This meed from miscreants makes them so rich
That law becomes lord and loyalty poor;
Unkindness is commander and kindness is banished.
But common sense shall come yet, together with conscience,
And make of law a laborer, such love shall arise."

PASSUS IV

"Stop," said the king, "I can suffer you no longer.
You shall settle your quarrel, and serve me together.
Kiss her," said the king, "Conscience, I command you!"
"No, by Christ," said Conscience, "banish me instead;
Unless Reason advise it I'd much rather die!"
Then the king said to Conscience, "Hear my command,
You must hasten to ride and bring Reason here.
Command that he come, my counsel to hear;
For he shall rule my realm and render best counsel
Of Meed and the others and what man she shall wed,
And account with you, Conscience, so help me Christ,
How you lead my people, the learned and the lay."
    "I am pleased with that promise," Conscience replied,
And rode away to Reason and whispered in his ear,
Gave him the king's message, and would have taken his leave.
"I shall prepare me to ride," said Reason, "wait just a moment."
And called Cato, his servant, courteous of speech:
"Set my saddle on Suffer-till-I-see-my-time,
And see you secure him well with sensible bands.
Hang a heavy bridle on him to hold his head low;
Yet he'll make many a neigh, before we come there."
    Then Conscience on his horse hastens away
And Reason rides with him, hurrying quickly.
But one Warren Wisdom and Witty his companion
Followed them fast, for they had much to do

In exchequer and chancery to discharge many duties;
And rode fast after Reason that he might advise them
How to save themselves from shame and from harm.
But Conscience came first to court, by a mile,
And walked beside Reason right to the king.
   Courteously the king came then to Reason;
Set him on the bench between himself and his son,
Where they spoke a great while wisely together.
   Then Peace came to parliament and brought a petition
Charging that Wrong had taken his wife,
And had ravished poor Rose, Reynald's beloved,
Deprived Margaret of her maidenhead despite her resistance.
"Both my geese and my pigs his underlings pillage;
I dare not for fear of him fight or complain.
He borrowed my bay horse and never brought him back,
Nor gave for him a farthing for anything I could do.
He maintains his own men to murder my servants;
Interferes with my fairs, fights while I'm trading;
Breaks down my barn door and bears away my wheat,
And gives only a tally for ten quarters of oats;
In addition he beats me and lies by my maiden.
Before him I am daunted, and don't dare to look up."
The king knew he spoke truth, for Conscience had told him.
   Then Wrong was afraid and Wisdom he sought;
To make peace with pence, he proffered him money,
And said, "Had I love of the king little would I care,
Though Peace and his power complained of me forever."
   Then Wisdom was worried, and Wit was as well,
Because Wrong had done so wicked a deed,
And he warned Wrong with this wise advice:
"Whoever works willfully will often make trouble.
I refer to yourself; you shall soon find it so.
Unless Meed can amend it, misfortune will follow;
Both your life and your land lie in the king's grace."
   Wrong then bowed to Wisdom and wept for his help;
His pence he offered handy-dandy to pay.
Then Wisdom and Wit went out together,
Took Lady Meed with them to win the king's mercy.
   Peace put forth his head; his forehead was bloody.
"Guiltless, God knows, this gash I received."
   Conscience and the king knew this to be true;
They knew well that Wrong was ever a wretch.
But Wisdom and Wit went eagerly about
To gain the king's judgment with gifts if they could.
   The king swore by Christ and by his crown also,

That Wrong should woe suffer for his wicked works.
He commanded a constable to cast him in irons:
"Seven years shall he never see his feet once."
"God knows," said Wisdom, "that would not be wise.
If he promise to amend let him make bail,
And be pledge for his wrongdoing and pay for his release,
And amend his misdeeds, and so everyone wins."
Wit agreed with this plan and proposed the same thing:
"Better payment for the plaintiff to lessen his pain,
Than a beating for our client with no benefit at all."
Then Meed became meek and mercy besought,
And offered Peace a present of purest red gold;
"Have this of me," she said, "to help heal your wound,
For I guarantee that Wrong won't hurt you again."
Then piteously Peace prayed to the king
To have mercy on that man who mistreated him often.
"Since he has promised amends as Wisdom advised him,
I forgive him his guilt with a good will.
If you give your assent, I will argue no further.
Meed made me amends; I can ask for no more."
"No," said the king then, "so God give me bliss,
Wrong goes not away until I know more;
If he leap lightly away he'll laugh at us all,
And then be the bolder to beat my poor servants.
Unless Reason show pity he stays in the stocks,
As long as I live unless more love redeem him."
Then some pleaded with Reason to have pity on that wretch,
And to counsel the king and Conscience as well;
Meed must be surety; this they besought.
"Counsel me not," said Reason, "to have compassion at all
Until lords and ladies all love the truth,
And Peronelle's fur be put in her closet,
Till cherishing children be chastising with rods,
Till the tales of entertainers be treated with scorn,
Till clerks and knights speak with more courtesy,
And repent of their ribaldry and repeat it no longer;
Till priests ponder their preaching and apply it to themselves,
And by their example inspire us to good;
Till Saint James be sought where I shall assign,
And no man go to Galicia unless he go forever;[1]
And all runners to Rome, because of robbers abroad,

[1] A criticism of the popular pilgrimages to the shrine of St. James in the province of Galicia.

Bear no silver overseas that shows the king's sign,
Neither groats nor gold engraved with the king's crown,
Upon forfeiture of that fee if they're discovered at Dover,
Unless it be a merchant or his man or messenger with letters,
Or provisor or priest whom the pope has promoted.
"By the cross," said Reason, "I shall have no compassion
While Meed has permission to plead in this hall.
But I may show you examples to explain how I see it.
For I say for myself that if it should be
That I were a crowned king with care of a realm,
No wrong in this world that I was aware of
Would be unpunished by my power on peril of my soul,
Nor get favors through gifts, so help me God!
Nor through meed have mercy, unless meekness demand it.
For *nullum malum*, the man, met with *inpunitum*,
and bade *nullum bonum* be *irremuneratum*.[1]
Let your confessor, sir king, construe this in English.
If you put this in action I'll pledge both my ears,
That Law shall be laborer and lead afield dung,
And Love shall lead your land as you surely would like."
Clerks who were confessors came quickly together
To construe this clause and its quaint grammar.
But when Reason explained it to the people around him,
There was no one in that hall neither greater nor less,
Who did not hold him master and Meed a mere wretch.
Love thought little of Meed, and laughed her to scorn,
And spoke out so loudly that Truth himself heard it:
"He who wishes to wed her because of her wealth,
If he be not a cuckold, cut off my nose."
Neither Warren Wisdom nor Witty his companion
Could utter a word to contradict Reason,
But stared in a study and stood still as beasts.
The king agreed in the end to the arguments of Reason
And repeated what Reason had rightfully shown;
"But it will be hard, I'm afraid, to bring it about,
And all my loyal people to lead so evenly."
"By him who hung on the cross," cried Reason to the king,
"Unless I rule thus your realm, rend out my ribs!
As long as Obedience be at my service."
"I assent," said the king, "by Saint Mary, my lady,

[1] Latin resembles Innocent III, *De Contemptu Mundi*: "That one is a just judge who leaves *no evil unpunished, and no good unrewarded*." See Nick Gray, *Modern Philology* 84 (1986): 55–56.

With the concurrence of my council of clerks and of earls.
But not readily, Reason, will you ride hence,
For as long as I live I will not allow it."
"I am ready," said Reason, "to remain with you always;
As long as Conscience be our counsellor, I care for none better."
"I grant that gladly," said the king, "God forbid he be absent;
And as long as I live let us all live together."

PASSUS V

The king and his knights went to the church
To hear Matins and Mass and have their meal after.
Then I woke from my sleep and was sorry, indeed,
That I had not slept soundly and seen something more.
Before travelling a furlong a faintness came on me;
I could go no foot farther for I needed more sleep.
I sat softly down, saying my creed,
And babbled on my beads; that put me to sleep.
Then I saw much more than I have described,
Of the field full of folk that I showed you before,
For Conscience with a cross came there to preach.
He pleaded with the people to have pity on themselves,
And proved that the pestilence was penalty for sin,
And that southwest wind on a Saturday evening
Was plainly for pride and for no other reason.
Pear trees and plum trees were puffed to the ground,
As a warning, sinners, that you should do better.
Beeches and broad oaks were blown to the earth,
And their roots were turned upward as a token of fear
That deadly sin before doomsday should destroy them all.[1]
Of this matter I might mumble forever,
But I say as I saw, so help me God!
How Conscience with a cross commenced then to preach.
He bade waster to work at what he knew best,
And earn what he spent with some kind of skill.
He pleaded with Peronelle to put away her fur

[1] The pestilence (or Black Death) began in 1348–49, but a second serious visitation occurred in 1361–62, which may be referred to here. There was a storm with disastrously high winds on Saturday evening, 15 January 1362, described in lines 14–20. The upside down trees of lines 18–20 are an iconographical feature, one of the fifteen signs of the Doom.

And keep it in her cupboard in case of need.
Thomas he taught to take two strong staves
And fetch home Felice from her public punishment.[1]
He warned Master Walter that his wife was to blame
That her hat cost a mark and his hood not a groat.
He charged these merchants to chasten their children:
"Don't indulge them with your wealth while they are young."
He prayed both priests and prelates together,
What they preach to the people they should practice themselves:
"If you live as you teach us, we will love you the better."
Then he counselled religious to follow their rule:
"Lest the king and his Council your communities harm,
And be steward in your stead till you are better disposed.
You that visit Saint James and saints at Rome,
Seek only Saint Truth, for he may save you all,
Who reigns with the Father and the Son,[2] his blessing be upon you."
Then Repentance ran forward and repeated his theme,
And made Will to weep water with his eyes.
Peronelle Proudheart prostrated herself,
Lay long before she looked up and "Lord, mercy," she cried
And promised to Him who created us all,
To unsew her new smock and insert a hair cloth
To punish her flesh which was so prone to sin:
"Never shall high heart rule me but humble I'll be,
And let myself be slandered, as I never did before.
Now I will be meek and mercy beseech
From all for whom I had envy in my heart."
Lecher said, "Alas!" and cried to our lady,
To beg God for mercy for his misdeeds,
Provided that on Saturdays, for seven years after,
He would drink with the duck and dine only once.
Envy with heavy heart asked for confession
And sorrowfully his guilt began to reveal.
As pale as a pellet, in a palsy he seemed,
Clad in clothing so coarse I can scarcely describe it:
A vest and a short coat a keen knife by his side;
From a friar's frock were the foresleeves.

---

[1] A scolding wife was punished by the ducking stool.

[2] Translates *Qui cum patre et filio*, resembling the formula with which sermons were often concluded. In this case it will be noticed that the formula "who with the Father and the Holy Spirit" is changed to read "the Father and the *Son*," thus suggesting that Saint Truth is to be identified with the Holy Spirit or third person of the Trinity.

As a leek that had lain long in the sun,
So he looked with his lean cheeks and his livid scowl.
His body was so swollen with wrath that he bit his lips,
And clenched his fist angrily, thinking to avenge himself
With works or with words when he saw his time.
"Venom or verjuice or vinegar I believe,
Roils in my belly or grows in my bowel.
Many days I can't do what a man ought to do,
Such gas in my gut growls before dinner.
    "I have a neighbor near me I have often annoyed,
Blamed behind his back to bring him to ruin.
To harm him by my power I pursued him with slander;
Lied about him to lords to make him lose silver;
Made his friends be his foes through my false tongue.
His grace and good fortune have given me pain.
Between him and his household I have fostered ill will;
Both his life and his limb were lost through my tongue.
When I meet him at market whom I hate most
I hail him as heartily as if I were his friend.
Since he is bolder than I, I dare not attack him;
But had I mastery and might, I would murder him at once!
    "When I come to the church and kneel by the cross,
To pray for the people, as the priest teaches,
On my knees I cry out that Christ give him sorrow
Who bore away my bowl and my tattered sheet.
Away from the altar my eyes turn to see
How Heyne has a new coat, and his wife another;
Then I wish it were mine and the whole cloth as well.[1]
I laugh when he loses, that lightens my heart,
But for his winnings I weep and bewail the time.
I condemn those who do ill and yet I do worse,
Wishing everyone in this world were my own servant;
And whoever has more than I, that angers my heart.
    Thus I live loveless like a wretched dog,
My breast is in turmoil from the bitterness of my bile;
No sugar nor other sweet thing can assuage it at all,
Nor medicinal mixtures remove it from my heart.
If confession could cleanse it I'd consider it a wonder."
    "Yes, easily," said Repentance, exhorting him to good;
"Sorrow for sins has saved many men."
"I am sorry," said Envy, "I am seldom otherwise,

[1] Envy wants the coat, as well as any cloth that may have been left over when it was made.

For it makes me angry that I may get no revenge."
    Then Avarice came; I can hardly describe him.
So hungry, so hollow, he looked like Sir Harvey.
He was beetle-browed and thick-lipped and bleary-eyed too;
Like a purse of leather hung his lean cheeks.
He wore a torn tunic at least twelve years old;
Unless a louse leap I can scarcely believe
He could cross over that cloth, it was so threadbare.
    "I was covetous," said this creature, "I'll acknowledge it here.
For some time I served Simon at the Oak
As his pledged apprentice overseeing his profit.
First I learned to lie, a leaf or two;
How to weigh wrongly was my first lesson.
To Winchester and Weyhill I went to the fair
With many kinds of merchandise as my master commanded;
But had not the grace of guile gone among my wares
They'd be unsold these seven years, so help me God!
Then I drew among drapers to study my primer:
How to stretch out the cloth and make it seem longer.
Among the rich fabrics I finished the lesson:
Basted them with a packing-needle, and pleated them together,
Put them in a press and pinned them therein,
Until ten yards or twelve were stretched to thirteen.
My wife was a weaver who made woolen cloth,
Spoke to the spinners to spin the wool fine.
The pound that she paid by weighed a quarter pound more
Than my own balance showed when I weighed as I should.
I bought her some barley; she brewed it to sell.[1]
Penny ale and dregs she poured together
For laborers and lowly folk who lay by themselves.
The best in my bed-chamber lay by the wall;
Whoever drank a draught of it paid for it dearly,
A gallon for a groat, God knows, no less,
When it came by the cup, such craft my wife used.
Rose the retailer was her right name;
She has been a huckster for eleven winters.
But I swear now, truly, that sin I'll forsake,
And never weigh wickedly nor falsify wares,
But wend my way to Walsingham and my wife will also,
And beg the cross at Bromholm to bring me out of debt."
    Now Glutton begins to go to confession,

[1] See R. H. Hilton, "Lords, Burgesses and Hucksters," *Past and Present* 97 (Nov. 1982): 3–15.

And trots off to church to tell all his sins.
Betty the brewster bade him good morning,
And then she asked him where he was going.
"To the church," said he, "to hear holy Mass,
And then I'll be absolved and sin no more."
"I have good ale, Glutton," said she, "Would you like a sip?"
"Do you have in your purse," said he, "any hot spices?"
"Yes, Glutton, my friend," said she. "God knows they're quite hot:
I have pepper and peony-seeds and a pound of garlic,
And a farthing worth of fennel seed, for fasting days."
Then Glutton goes in and great oaths come after.
Cicely the seamstress sat on the bench,
Wat the warrener, and his wife also,
Tom the tinker and two of his servants,
Hick, the horse dealer, and Hugh, the needle seller,
Clarice of Cock Lane and the clerk of the church,
Sir Peter Pray-well and Peronelle of Flanders,
Davie, the ditch digger, and a dozen others;
A fiddler, a ratcatcher, a raker of Cheapside,
A ropemaker, a retainer, and Rose the dish-seller;
And auctioneers aplenty early in the morning
Give Glutton with glad cheer good ale to drink.
Clement the cobbler cast off his cloak,
And playing "at the new fair" he put it up for sale;
Hick, the horse dealer, flung his hood down,
And bade Bart the butcher be on his side.
Then tradesmen were appointed to appraise the merchandise;
Whoever had the hood should have amends for the cloak.[1]
Rapidly they rose up and whispered together,
And put a price on the goods apart from the others;
Oaths were aplenty, whoever could hear them.
They could not in conscience come to agreement
Till Robin the rope-maker was told to arise
And named as an umpire to avoid a debate.
Hick the horse dealer was handed the cloak
On condition that Clement should fill up the cup,
Have the horse dealer's hood and hold himself served.
He who changed his mind soonest should stand up at once
And greet good Sir Glutton with a gallon of ale.
There was laughing and leering and "Let the cup go round!"

---

[1] The cloak given to Hick was more valuable; hence Clement, who got the hood, had his cup filled to balance the trade (lines 180–82). The game was designed to provide opportunities for frequent filling of the cup (183–88).

Bargains and beverages began to arise
And they sat there till evensong and sang for a while,
Until Glutton had gulped down a gallon and a quarter.
He passed two quarts of water in the space of a prayer,[1]
And blew the round horn at the base of his spine.
All that heard that loud horn held their noses afterward
And wished it were plugged up with a tuft of furze.
No strength had he standing till he found his staff:
Then began he to go like a gleeman's bitch,[2]
Sometimes to one side and sometimes to the other,
Like fowlers who set lines to ensnare their birds.
When he drew near the door his bleary eyes dimmed;
He stumbled on the threshold and threw himself down.
With all the woe of the world, his wife and his daughter,
Bore him home to his house and helped him to bed.
After all this surfeit, a fever he had,
And slept Saturday and Sunday till the sun went to rest.
    When he woke from his sleep, and wiped his dull eyes,
The first word that he spoke was, "Where is the cup?"
His wife warned him then of wickedness and sin.
Then the wretch was ashamed, and scratched both his ears,
And began to cry loudly and make lamentation
For the wicked life he had lived so long,
And vowed to fast despite hunger or thirst:
"Not even fish on Friday shall be food for my gut
Until Abstinence my aunt has given me leave;
And yet I have hated her all of my life."
    Sloth in his sorrow fell down in a swoon
Till *Vigilance*,[3] the watcher, threw water at his eyes,
Flung it in his face and fervently cried,
Saying, "Beware of despair, that will surely betray you.
'I am sorry for my sins,' say to yourself,
And beat yourself on the breast and beg for God's grace.
There is no guilt so great that his goodness is not more."
    Then Sloth sat up and signed himself quickly
And made a promise to God to forego his foul sloth:
"For seven years every Sunday, unless sickness prevent it,
I shall go before dawn to the dear church
And hear Matins and Mass as if I were a monk;
No ale after meals shall ever detain me

---

[1] The original line 189 reads: He pisside a potel, in a *pater noster* while.
[2] I.e., like a guide dog (minstrels were often blind).
[3] *Vigilate*, "Watch" (Mark 13:37).

Till I have heard Vespers, this I vow to the cross.
And yet I promise to repay, from whatever I possess,
All that I wrongfully won since I reached the use of reason.
Though my livelihood fail, I will not delay
Till each one is repaid before I pass hence;
And with the rest that remains, by the rood of Chester,
I shall seek holy Truth before I see Rome!"
    Robert the robber looked on *Repay-what-thou-owest*,[1]
And having not a penny, piteously he wept.
Yet this wretched sinner said to himself:
"Christ, who on Calvary died on the cross,
When Dismas,[2] my brother, begged you for grace
(And you had mercy on that man for *remembrance's*[3] sake)
Your will be done on me as I have deserved,
To have hell forever if there were no hope.
Have pity on this robber, with no means to repay,
Nor any thought of earning by any skill that I know;
But for your great mercy, forgiveness I seek:
Damn me not at doomsday for the wrong I have done."
What happened to this felon I cannot rightly say;
But I know he wept copiously and cried through his tears,
And acknowledged his guilt to Christ once again,
Saying Penitence his pike he would polish like new,
And leap with it over land for the rest of his life;
For he had lain by *Latro*,[4] Lucifer's kin.
    Thousands of people then thronged together,
Weeping and wailing for their wicked deeds,
Praying to Christ and to His pure mother,
For grace to seek Truth, if God grant that they may!

PASSUS VI

Few were so wise as to know the way thither,
But they blustered forth like beasts over valleys and hills,
Till finally they met a man on the way
Appareled like a pagan, in pilgrim's guise.

---

[1] *Reddite*, "Make restitution" (Rom. 13:7).

[2] Dismas was the name assigned to the anonymous penitent thief (see Luke 23:40–42) in the apocryphal *Gospel of Nicodemus*.

[3] *Memento*, "Remember me" (Luke 23:42).

[4] Latro, "Thief" from a reference to the thieves (*latronibus*) in Luke 23:39–43.

He bore a staff that was bound with a broad strip of cloth:
Like the climbing woodbine it was wound about;
A bag and a bowl he bore by his side.
A hundred small ampules were pinned on his hat,
Signs of Sinai and shells of Galicia,
Crosses on his cloak and the keys of Rome,
And the vernicle in front for everyone to know,
And see by his signs what shrines he had sought.[1]
These folk asked him courteously from whence he had come.
    "From Sinai," he said, "and from the holy sepulchre;
From Bethlehem and Babylon, I have been in both;
In Armenia and Alexandria and other such places.
You may see by my signs which are set on my hat,
That I've walked far and wide in wet weather and in dry,
And have sought holy saints for the health of my soul."
"Do you know of a saint," said they, "that men call Truth?
Can you show us the path to the place where he dwells?"
"No, so help me God," said the man then,
"I never saw palmer with pike or knapsack
Ask me about him until now in this place."
    "Peter!" said a plowman, and put forth his head.
"I know him as naturally as a clerk knows his books.
Clean conscience and common sense conducted me to him
And then made me promise to serve him forever,
Both to sow and to plant while I've power to work.
I've been his follower all these forty winters.
I sowed all his seed and attended his beasts,
And cared for his corn, carried it to the barn,
Dug and delved, did what he asked,
Within and without watched over his profit.
No laborer in his land does he love better,
For though I say it myself, he is pleased with my service.
I receive a fair income and at times even more;
He is the promptest payer that poor men could have.
His servants have their wages before the sun sets.
He is lowly as a lamb and lovely of speech,
And if you want to know where he now dwells,
I will point out the path right to his place."
"Yes, Piers," said the pilgrims, and offered to pay him.

---

[1] The pilgrim wears emblems showing where he has travelled: Canterbury (ampules), Sinai ("signs" unspecified), St. James in Galicia (shells), the Holy Land (crosses), and Rome (cross-keys and vernicle). For an earlier pejorative reference to the shrine of St. James, see above, IV 109–10.

"No, on my soul's peril," began Piers to swear,
"I'll accept not a cent, for Saint Thomas' shrine;[1]
Truth would love me the less a long time after.
But you who want to go there, this is the way:
You must go through Meekness, both men and women,
Till you come to Conscience so that Christ know the truth,
That you love Him more dearly than the life in your hearts,
And then next your neighbor; do nothing to him
But what you would want others to do unto you.[2]
"Then turn by a brook Be-humble-of-speech;
Go on till you find a ford Honor-your-fathers.
Wade in that water, wash yourself well,
And you shall leap more lightly for the rest of your life.
Soon you shall see Swear-not-without-need,
And-especially-not-in-vain-the-name-of-God-almighty.
Then you shall come to a croft but do not go in;
The place is called Covet-not-men's-possessions-nor-their-wives,
Nor-any-of-their-servants-for-that-might-distress-them;
Look you break no branch there, but it be your own.
Two stocks there stand, but don't even pause;
They are Slay-not and Steal-not; slip by them both.
Leave them on your left hand and do not look back,
And hold well your holy day solemnly till evening.
Then you shall pass by a barrow, Bear-no-false-witness,
Which is hedged in with florins and other fees aplenty:
Pluck no plant there on peril of your soul.
Then you shall see Say-the-truth-so-that-it-be-done-
And-take-care-that-you-lie-not-at-any-one's-command.
"Then you shall come to a court as clear as the sun:
The moat is of Mercy encircling the manor,
All the walls are of wit to keep self-will out,
The battlements are Christendom, mankind to preserve,
Buttressed with Believe-or-you-cannot-be-saved;
All the houses are roofed, the halls and the chambers,
Not with lead, but with love, as brothers of one womb.
The tower where Truth is reaches up to the sun;

---

[1] The shrine of St. Thomas à Becket at Canterbury, the most popular (and wealthy) shrine in Britain, and the goal of the pilgrims in Chaucer's *Canterbury Tales*.

[2] The Great Commandment (Matt. 22:37–40), to which is added the golden rule. The passage following these lines, of course, provides an allegorical map of the Ten Commandments (Exod. 20:3–17). Line 49 is difficult, but may be paraphrased: "until you come to an inner awareness (Conscience) of what God requires of you, which Christ, who knows our thoughts (Matt. 9:4), will recognize."

He may do with the day-star whatever he wills;
Death dare not do any deed he forbids.
"Grace is the gate-keeper, a good man, indeed.
His assistant is Amend-you; many a man knows him.
Tell him this text: 'Truth knows the truth:
I performed the penance imposed by the priest;
I am sorry for my sins and so shall I always,
Whenever I think of them though I were pope.'
Bid Amend-you go meekly and beg of his master,
That he open the wicket which the angel shut,
When Adam and Eve ate the fatal fruit.
For he keeps the key though the king sleep.
And if Grace grant you permission to go in this way
You shall see Truth himself sitting in your heart,
Teaching you to love Him and keep all His laws.
"But be wary of Wrath that villain most wicked,
For he is envious of Him who sits in your heart
And pushes you to pride in praising yourself.
The boldness of your good deeds may make you turn blind,
And you'll be driven out as the early dew,[1] and the door closed,
Locked with a key to keep you outside,
Perhaps for a hundred years before you may enter.
Thus you may lose His love, loving yourself too well,
But get it again by grace and by no other gift.
"Seven sisters there are who always serve Truth,
And are portresses at the postern-gates that are part of this place.
One is called Abstinence, Humility another,
Charity and Chastity are her chief maidens;
Patience and Peace help many people;
Liberality, the lady, lets in very many.
Whoever is kin to these sisters—so help me God!—
Is wonderfully welcome and very well received;
And unless you're related to some of these seven,
It is very hard, by my head, for any of you there
To gain entrance at any gate unless grace be the more."
"By Christ," said a cut-purse, "I have no kin there!"
"Nor I," said an ape-keeper, "for aught that I know!"
"God knows," said a cake-maker, "if this be true,
I'd go no foot farther, for any friar's preaching."
"Yes," said Piers the plowman, and pressed him to go.
"Mercy is a maiden there who has might over all;

[1] "Therefore they shall be as the morning cloud, and as the early dew that passeth away. . . ." (Hos. 13:3).

She is kin to all sinners and so is her son;
And with the help of those two (hope for no other),
You might get grace there, if you go in time."

PASSUS VII

"This way would be perilous had we no guide
To attend us on foot until we arrived."
Said Perkin the plowman, "By Peter the apostle,
I have a half-acre by the highway;
Had I plowed that half-acre, so help me God,
I would go with you gladly until you got there."
"This were a long delay," said a lady in a veil,
"What work shall we women do all that while?"
"Some shall sew sacks so the wheat won't be spilled;
And you wives that have wool, work it diligently,
Spin it speedily, spare not your fingers,
Unless it be holy day or else holy eve.
Look after your linen and labor with care,
Take note of the plight of the needy and the naked,
Give them clothes for the cold, for Truth so commands.
I shall furnish them food unless the crops fail,
As long as I live, for the love of our Lord.
And you lovely ladies with your long fingers,
Who have fine cloth and silk, sew while you can
Chasubles for chaplains, churches to honor.
And all manner of men, who must eat to live,
Help those work swiftly who supply you with food."
"By Christ," said a knight then, "you counsel us best!
Yet on this theme, truly, I never was taught.
But instruct me," the knight said, "and I'll soon learn to plow."
"By Saint Paul," said Piers, "since you proffer so humbly,[1]
I shall work hard and sweat and sow for us both,
And labor for your love all my lifetime,
If you promise to protect Holy Church and myself
From wasters and wicked men who would seek to destroy us.
And hunt with great hardiness for hares and for foxes,

[1] Piers here addresses the knight using the familiar form of the second person pronoun, "for *thou* profrist *the* so lowe," perhaps suggesting that in some sense the plowman and knight are equals, even though they are differentiated as regards social function. The B version reads, "*ye* profre *yow* so faire" (C omits).

For boars and for bucks that break down men's hedges,
And fetch a few falcons to kill the wild fowl,
For they come to my field and feed on my wheat."
Courteously the knight uttered these words:
"By my power, Piers, I pledge you my troth,
To fulfill this agreement while I may stand."
"One more point," then said Piers, "I pray you also:
Do not trouble any tenant unless Truth will approve;
And if poor men should proffer you presents or gifts,
Take them not, lest by chance you may not deserve them;
For you will yield them again at the end of a year,
In a perilous place: purgatory it is called.
And punish not your peasants, you'll prosper the better.
Be truthful in speech, and despise idle tales
Lacking wisdom or wit to edify your workmen.
Have no regard for ribalds, nor relish their tales,
And especially at meals avoid all such men.
They are the devil's tale-tellers, take my word for it!"
"I agree, by Saint James!" said the knight then,
"To work by your word while my life endures."
"And I'll clothe myself," said Perkin, "in pilgrim's garb,
And go with you on the way until we find Truth."
He put on his clothes, well patched and mended,
His leggings and his cuffs to keep out the cold,
And hung his hopper from his neck, instead of a knapsack:
"A bushel of bread-corn bring to me here;
I will sow it myself and soon I'll go with you.
Whoever helps me to plow or works in any way,
Shall have leave, by our Lord, to glean here in harvest-time[1]
And make him merry with the leavings, whoever may grumble.
All kinds of craftsmen, holding to the truth,
I shall find them their food who faithfully live,
Except Jack the juggler, and Janet of the brothels,
And Robert the ribald, for his raunchy words.
Truth taught me this once and bade me tell others:
From the Book of Life blot them,[2] bother not with them,
Nor may Holy Church take from them any tithes at all.

---

[1] "Shal have be oure lord the more hire in hervist" (A). This may be one of those rare cases where the A text is corrupt, and B preserves the original reading: "Shal haue leue, bi owre lord, to lese here in heruest" (B VI 68), used here as a basis for the translation.

[2] "Let them be blotted out of the book of the living; and with the just let them not be written." Ps. 69:28 (V 68:29).

They have escaped by good fortune; now may God amend them."[1]
Dame-work-while-there's-time is the name of Piers' wife;
His daughter is Do-what-is-right-or-your-dear-mother-will-beat-you;
His son's name is Suffer-your-superiors-to-have-their-own-way,
And-condemn-them-not-for-if-you-do-you-shall-pay-for-it-dearly;
Let-God-determine-all-things-for-so-His-word-teaches.[2]
"Because I am old and have enough of my own,
To penance and to pilgrimage I will pass with these others.
Before going I wish to write my last will.
"*In the name of God, amen.*[3] I make it myself:
My soul shall He have Who best has deserved it,
And shall defend it from the fiend, for so I believe,
Till I come to His accounting as my creed teaches,
To have release and remission, in that reckoning I trust.
The church shall have my body and keep all my bones;
For of my grain and my goods he demanded the tithe;
I paid it all promptly on peril of my soul.
He is bound now, I hope, to have me in mind,
And remember me in his Mass, among all good Christians.[4]
My wife shall have what I earned with honesty, no more,
And distribute it to my friends and to my dear children,
For though I die on this day my debts are all paid;
I gave back what I borrowed before going to bed,
And whatever remains, by the rood of Chester,
I will worship Truth with, throughout my life,
And be his pilgrim at the plow for the sake of poor men.
My plow-foot shall be my pike and push at the roots,
And help my coulter to cut and enclose the furrows."[5]
Now are Piers and the pilgrims gone to the plow.
To prepare this half-acre many men help;
Ditchers and delvers dig up the ridges.
Then Perkin was pleased and eagerly praised them.
Other workmen there were who worked very hard;
Each man in his way did what he could;

---

[1] I.e., from Ps. 69:28 we may infer that these reprobates are exempt from tithes—bully for them! But in all seriousness their immortal souls are at risk: may God amend them before it is too late.

[2] Rom. 12:19 (Deut. 32:35).

[3] *In dei nomine, amen*: The standard beginning of a last will and testament. "I make it myself" means "I compose this in my own hand."

[4] In describing the mutual obligations of church and parishioner, Piers uses the masculine pronoun ("he") because he seems to have in mind the parish priest as representative of the church here.

[5] See Kane, *A-Version*, 447, note to line 96.

And some, to please Perkin, pulled up the weeds.
At the hour of prime Piers let the plow stand,
While he witnessed himself who worked the best;
He would hire them there-after when harvest-time came.
Then some men sat down and sang at the ale house,
And helped plow the half acre with "hey trolly lolly."
"By the Prince of Paradise!" said Piers then in anger,
"Unless you rise in a hurry and hasten to work,
No grain that grows here will gladden you in need;
And though you die in distress, the devil have him who cares!"
Then the fakers were afraid and feigned they were blind.
And some laid their legs askew, as such shirkers can,
And pleaded with Piers in these piteous words:
"We have no limbs to labor with, thanks be to our Lord,
But we pray for you, Piers, and for your plow as well,
That God by His grace will multiply your grain,
And repay you for the alms you have given us here.
For we may neither sweat nor slave, such sickness afflicts us."
"If it be true what you say," said Piers, "I shall soon see it!
You are wasters, I know, and Truth knows the truth.
I am his loyal servant and so ought to warn him,
That such wasters in this world his workmen destroy.
You eat what they should eat who plow for us all.
But Truth himself shall teach you how to drive well his team,
How to sow and to plant and protect all his produce,
Chase crows from his corn and care for his beasts,
Or you shall eat barley bread and drink from the brook.
But those who are blind or broken-legged, or who lie bedridden
Shall share what I have, so help me God,
Till God, of His grace, grant that they arise.[1]
"Anchorites and hermits who keep to their cells,
Shall share in my alms all the while I live,
Each noon have enough, but no more till the morrow,
Lest his flesh and the fiend befoul his pure soul.
Once at noon is enough for those engaged in no labor;
His soul is safer who sips not too often."
Then Waster arose, ready for a fight;
To Piers the Plowman he proffered his glove.
A Breton, a bragger, boasted as well,
And bade him go piss with his plow, bald-pated shrew.
"Whether you will it or not we'll have what we want,
And make away when we wish with your meat and your flour,

---

[1] Cf. Mark 2:11.

And have a feast for ourselves in spite of your threats!"
Then Piers the plowman complained to the knight,
To protect him as promised from profitless wretches,
From wasters who lie in wait the winners to ruin.
Courteously the knight then, according to his nature,
Gave warning to Waster and admonished him further,
"Or you'll suffer the limit of the law, I swear by my order."
"I was not used to work," said Waster, "I will not begin now."
And made light of the law, and less of the knight,
Counted Piers and his plow no more than a pea,
And menaced him and his men when next they would meet.
"Now, by peril of my soul," said Piers, "I shall punish you all!"
And whooped after Hunger who heard him at once:
"Avenge me on these wasters, who are destroying this world!"
Then Hunger in haste seized Waster by the middle,
Squeezed his stomach so tightly that there were tears in his eyes,
And buffeted the Breton on both his cheeks,
Till he looked like a lantern for the rest of his life.
He gave the knaves such a knock, he nearly burst their bellies:
Had not Piers with a pease-loaf prayed him to leave off,
And with a batch of beans stepped in between them,
And hit Hunger with it on both of his lips,
So that he bled into his body a bowl full of gruel;
Had not the physician at first denied him water
To retard the barley-bread and the ground beans,
They'd be dead this day, and buried all warm.[1]
Then sluggards, for fear, flew to the barns
And flapped grain with flails from morning till night,
So that Hunger did not dare to do them more harm,
For a potfull of peas that Piers had just made.
A horde of hermits took hold of their spades,
And dug dirt and dung to drive Hunger out.
The blind and the bedridden were cured by the thousands,
Who feigned blindness and broken legs by the highway;
Hunger had healed them with a hot cake.
The limbs of lame men were suddenly lithe,
And they became herdsmen to care for Piers' beasts,
And prayed that for love they might live there with Piers,
For they wanted his grain to drive Hunger away.

---

[1] A complex allegorical action here depicts the effect of starvation on the human body, and takes the form of an attack by Hunger on Waster and the Breton. Piers saves the victims' lives by feeding Hunger beans; a physician restricts the intake of fluids so that the sudden end of the enforced fasting will not prove fatal.

Piers was proud of their efforts and put them to work,
Gave them meat and money as they might deserve.
Then Piers had pity and prayed Hunger to go
Home to his own abode and abide there forever.
"And yet I pray you," said Piers, "before you pass hence,
Concerning vagabonds and beggars, what is best to be done?
For I know well, when you go, they will work very little;
Because of misfortune they are friendly and mild,
And for want of good food they work very hard.
Yet they are my brothers, for God bought us all.
Truth taught me once to love them each one,
And help them in all things if they have need.
Yet would I know if you knew what way were best,
And how I might master them and move them to work."
"Hear now," said Hunger, "and heed this wisdom:
Bold beggars and wastrels who can work for their food,
With hound's bread and horse bread hold up their hearts,
And ply them with beans, lest their bellies swell.[1]
And if they complain, bid them go work,
And they shall sup the sweeter when they have deserved it.
And if you find any fellows whom fortune has injured
With fire, or false folk, try to befriend them,
Comfort them with kindness for Christ's love in heaven;
Love them and lend to them as the law of nature wills.
And all kinds of people whom you discover,
Who are needy or naked and have nothing to spend,
With meat or with money make them fare better,
With work or with word while you are here.
Make you friends with these, as Saint Matthew teaches."[2]
"I would not grieve God," said Piers, "for all the gold in the ground.
May I do without sin what you have said?"
"Yes, I assure you," said Hunger, "or else Scripture lies.

---

[1] For those who refuse to work a minimal diet is prescribed, just enough to prevent the swelling of the belly that is a sign of famine.

[2] "Make unto you friends of the mammon of iniquity" (Luke 16:9), from the parable of the unjust steward in the gospel of Luke (not Matthew, as the text says). This parable is traditionally associated with advocacy of charitable works: the steward seeks the friendship of his lord's debtors, "that when I shall be removed from the stewardship, they may receive me into their houses" (16:4), which Jesus interprets for his disciples, "Make unto you friends of the mammon of iniquity, that when you shall fail, they may receive you into everlasting dwellings" (16:9). Here the Douay translators add a footnote: "By this we see, that the poor servants of God, whom we have relieved by our alms, may hereafter, by their intercession, bring our souls to heaven."

Go to Genesis, the giant,[1] progenitor of all:
'In sweat and through effort you shall earn what you eat
And labor for your livelihood,' for our Lord so commanded.
And Wisdom says the same; I saw it in the Bible:
'Unwilling, because of the cold, to cultivate a field,
The sluggard shall go begging, his hunger unabated.'[2]
Matthew, with the man's face, mouthed these words:
One servant had a talent, and since he would not use it,
He was hated by his master evermore after,
Who took away his talent, since he wouldn't work,
And gave it to him who already had ten.
And then he said sternly so his servants could hear:
'He who has shall have, to help where there is need,
And he who has not, shall have not, and no one will help him;
And he who hopes to have more, shall have it taken away.'[3]
For Common Sense would that each one work,
Whether teaching or tilling, or working with one's hands,
Active life or contemplative; Christ wills it also.
For so says the psalter in the psalm 'Blessed are all':
He who wins his food here with the work of his hands,
God gives them His blessing that gain thus their livelihood."[4]
"Yet I beseech you," said Piers, "for charity's sake,
If you know any medicine, teach me my friend,
For some of my servants are sick for a while:
A whole week they don't work, such stomach pains they have."
"I know well," said Hunger, "what sickness ails them.
They have eaten too much, which makes them groan so.
But I warn you," said Hunger, "if you want to be healthy,
Not to drink any day until you have dined.
Eat not, I tell you, until Hunger overtakes you,
And sends you his sauce to appeal to your palate.
Keep some until supper and sit not too long;
Arise before Appetite has eaten his fill.
Let not Sir Surfeit sit at your table;

---

[1] Gen. 3:19 (largest book of the Bible, except for Psalms).

[2] Prov. 20:4 (one of the biblical books of Wisdom).

[3] Matt. 24:14–30 (Luke 19:12–27), the parable of the talents. "Matthew with the man's face" refers to the traditional identification of "the third living creature having the face, as it were, of a man" in Revelation 4:7 with the evangelist Matthew. Similarly the lion was Mark, the calf Luke, and the eagle John.

[4] Ps. 128 (V 127) is identified by its opening words, *Beati omnes* ("Blessed are all"). Verse 2 of this psalm, "For thou shalt eat the labours of thy hands: blessed art thou, and it shall be well with thee," is paraphrased in lines 235–36.

Love him not; he's a lecher, and loose in his speech,
And his gut is always greedy for every kind of food.
And if you follow this diet, I dare pledge my ears,
That Physic for food shall sell his furred hood,
And his Calabrian cloak with its buttons of gold,
And be fain, by my faith, to forfeit his practice,
And learn to labor on the land lest his livelihood fail.
There are more liars than leeches; may our Lord amend them!
They make men die through their potions before destiny wills it."
"By Saint Paul!" said Piers, "these are profitable words;
This is a lovely lesson; our Lord repay you for it!
Now go when you will, and good luck go with you."
"I promise you," said Hunger, "I will not proceed hence
Before I have dined this day and had something to drink."
"I've no penny," said Piers, "to purchase chickens,
Nor any piglets nor geese, only two green cheeses,
A few curds and cream and an oaten cake,
A loaf of beans and bran, baked for my children.
And I say, by my soul, I have no salt bacon,
Nor any eggs, by Christ, to make you a grill.
But I've parsley and onions and plenty of kale,
And a cow and a calf, and a cart-mare
To draw dung to pasture while the drought lasts.
By this means I must live until Lammas time.
By then I hope to have a harvest in my croft;
Then I'll prepare you a dinner that should please you well."
All the poor people went to fetch pea-pods;
Beans and baked apples they brought in their aprons,
Spring onions and chervils and many ripe cherries,
And proffered Piers this present to please Hunger a while.
Hunger ate this in haste and hankered for more.
Then these folk out of fear fetched him many
Green onions and peas, in an effort to appease him,
Until harvest drew near and new corn came to market.
Then the folk made a feast and fed Hunger the best;
With good ale and good food they got him to sleep.
And then Waster would not work but wandered about;
Nor any beggar eat bread that had beans in it,
Only very fine pastries made from pure wheat.
Nor would they drink any half-penny ale,
But the best and the brownest that brew-wives sell.
Laborers without land who live by their hands
Deign not to dine on day-old produce.
No penny-ale will please them nor piece of bacon,
Only fresh flesh or fish that was fried

Hot and even hotter, lest their stomachs be chilled.[1]
Unless very well paid, they will complain,
Bewailing the time they were made workmen,
And then curse the king and all of his council
For providing such laws to punish those who labor.
But while Hunger was in charge no one would chide,
Nor strive against the statute,[2] so stern was his glance.
I warn you workmen, earn while you may;
For Hunger hitherward hastens to return;
He shall awaken through water to punish wasters;
Before five years are finished, such famine shall arise,
Through floods and foul weather, that fruit trees shall fail,
And so says Saturn, who sends you this warning.

PASSUS VIII

Truth heard tell of this, and sent word to Piers
To take his team, and till the earth,
And procured him a pardon *from punishment and guilt*,[3]
For him and his heirs, evermore after;
And bade him keep himself at home and cultivate his fields,
And all who assist him to sow or to plow,
Or any kind of craftsman who might come to his aid,
Should have part in that pardon that the pope granted.
Kings and knights who care for Holy Church,
And rightfully rule the realm and the people,
Shall have pardon to pass through purgatory soon,
With the patriarchs in paradise to praise God forever.
Bishops who bless and know both the laws

[1] "And *chaud* and *plus chaud*, for chillyng of here mawe." Pretentious laborers, in time of plenty, use French phrases to order their dish "done" or "well done."

[2] Reference is to the Statute of Laborers, designed to freeze wages in the period following the plague (1348–49) when the shortage of workers caused wages to increase sharply. Frequent re-enactment of this statute indicates how difficult it was to enforce.

[3] Latin *a pena et a culpa*, "from punishment and guilt." In a normal pardon, this would be an excessive claim, since only God can remit the guilt of sin. But this pardon comes ultimately from Truth (=God), and for those who meet its severe conditions (see Latin following line 94 below) there will be no punishment *and no guilt*. The satire on conventional pardons in this passus has often eluded modern readers of the poem, especially those who seek to link its significance to later versions of the text (B and C) as yet unwritten when A was circulating. See also line 21.

Attend to one law and teach men the other,[1]
Bearing both on their back as their banner displays,
And preach to their parsons the peril of sin,
How the scabby sheep shall yet save their wool:
They have pardon with the apostles when they pass hence,
And at the day of doom shall dine at their table.
   Merchants, in the margin, had many years' indulgence
But the pope would not free them *from punishment and guilt*,
For they kept not their holydays as Holy Church teaches,
And they swore by their souls, so help them God,
Against clean conscience, to sell their goods.
   But under his seal Truth sent them a letter,
And bade them buy boldly what they liked best,
Then sell it again and save all the profit,
Build hospitals with it to help those who are ill;
Roads that are rutted they must quickly rebuild,
And repair all the bridges that are broken down,
Help maidens to marry or make them religious;
Poor widows who wish not to be wedded again,
Must be provided with food, for our Lord's love in heaven;
Send scholars to school or to study some skill,
Restore religious orders, and improve their endowments:
"And I shall send you myself Saint Michael my angel,
So no devil shall harm you, whenever you die,
For I shall send your souls safe into heaven,
And before the face of my father, fashion your seats.
Usury and avarice and oaths I forbid,
That no guile go with you, but only the straight truth."
Then the merchants were merry, and wept for pure joy,
And gave Will for his writing warm woolen clothes;
Because he copied thus their clause, they accorded him great meed.
   Men of law had the least, for they are all literate,
And should know what the Psalter and Wisdom both say:[2]
   He that hath not . . . taken bribes against the innocent.
   From kings and princes their payment shall come.

---

[1] Reference is to canon and civil law, governing respectively church and state in the Middle Ages.

[2] The first quotation is from Ps. 15:5 (V 14:5) and answers the question, "Lord, who shall dwell in thy tabernacle? or who shall rest in thy holy hill?" (15:1). Conscience earlier invoked this psalm (A III 219), and its importance for the *Visio* is pointed out by Clergy in B XIII 125–26. The source of the second is *Ecclesiasticus* 38:2 and its gloss. See John A. Alford, *Modern Philology* 81 (1984): 278–79. Also consult Alford's *Piers Plowman: A Guide to the Quotations* (1992) for the most recent information on all three versions. The promises of Ps. 15 are alluded to in lines 53–54.

From princes and prelates their profit should arise,
And from the poor people no penny should they take.
But he who practices his profession and speaks for a poor man
Who is innocent and needy and has injured no one,
Comforts him in his care, covets not his goods,
But for love of our Lord explains the law for him,
No devil at his death shall harm him in the least,
For his soul shall be safe, and so says the psalter.
But to buy water, or wind, or wit (which is third),
Scripture never intended; God knows this is true.
These three as servants have been sent to us freely
To wax and to wane, wherever God wills.
His pardon in purgatory is paltry, I trust,
Who takes profit from poor men for pleading their case.
You advocates and lawyers, you know I don't lie;
Since you see that is so, aspire to what is best.
    All living laborers who live by their hands,
Who justly receive, and justly earn,
And live in love and in law, lowly of heart,
Had the same absolution that Piers had received.
    Beggars and alms-seekers are not in the pardon,
Unless their reason for begging is based on the truth.
For he who begs or seeks alms, unless he have need,
Is as false as the fiend and defrauds the true needy,
And deceives the giver against his will.
They live not in love, nor have respect for the law.
They do not wed any woman that they have to do with,
But whinnying like wild beasts, they mingle together
And bring forth poor babes who are branded as bastards.
Their back or their bones they break in their youth,
And with their infants they ask alms, evermore after.[1]
There are more misshapen among them, whoever takes heed,
Than among all other men who wander on earth.
Those who live their lives thus may well loathe the time
That they were begotten when they go hence.
    But white-haired old men, helpless with age,
And women with child, unable to work,
The blind and bedridden and those with bones broken,
Who take misfortune meekly, as most lepers do,

[1] Readers of Charles Johnson's novel *Middle Passage* (New York: Athenaeum, 1990) will remember that when Illinois and his companion Squibb went ashore at a west African trading post they "tossed coins to beggars crippled at birth by their parents to make them better panhandlers. . . ."(60).

Have as full a pardon as the plowman himself.
For love of their low hearts our Lord has granted them
Their penance and purgatory upon this pure earth.[1]
"Piers," said a priest then, "your pardon I must read;
I will interpret each clause and explain it in English."
And Piers, at his request, unfolded the pardon,
And I, behind both, beheld the whole text.
In two lines it lay and not one letter more,
And was written in these words, in witness of Truth:[2]
Et qui bona egerunt, ibunt in vitam eternam;
Qui vero mala, in ignem eternum.
"Peter," said the priest then, "No pardon is here,
Only 'do well and have well and God will have your soul,
And do evil and have evil and hope for nothing else
Than that after your death to hell you shall go.' "
And Piers, in pure anger, pulled it asunder,
And said, *Though I should walk in the midst of the shadow of death, I will fear no evils, for thou art with me*[3]
"I shall cease from my sowing," said Piers, "and work not so hard,
Nor be so busy anymore about earning my bread.
Of prayer and of penance my plow shall be hereafter,
I shall frown at what I smiled at though my sustenance fail.
The prophet ate his bread in penance and in weeping,
As the psalter reminds us, and so did many others;
He who loves God with loyalty will have a full life:[4]
My tears have been my bread day and night.
And unless Luke is lying another lesson he teaches,
That we should not be so busy about what we eat.
Be not solicitous,[5] he says in his gospel,
And uses an example to make us understand.
Who provides for the birds when the winter winds blow?
When frost covers the fields, they must have their food.
They have no barn to go to, yet God provides for them."

---

[1] See Matt. 5:3–12. The poor who hold fast to their integrity amid suffering are exempt from the need for penitential instruments such as the pardons offered to sinners during this period.

[2] Latin is from the Athanasian Creed: "and those who have done good shall go into life eternal; and those who have done evil, into everlasting fire," paraphrased by the priest in lines 96–98.

[3] Ps. 23:4 (V 22:4).

[4] Ps. 42:3 (V 41:4); compare Ps. 34:10 (V 33:11), and Luke 1:53.

[5] Luke 12:22 (Matt. 6:25), "Be not solicitous for your life, what you shall eat, nor for your body, what you shall put on." Lines 111–13 are a paraphrase of Matt. 6:26.

"What!" said the priest to Piers, "Peter, it seems to me
That you have a little learning; who taught you your letters?"
"Abstinence the abbess the alphabet taught me,
And Conscience came after, and completed the work."
"Were you a priest, Piers," said he, "you might preach when
you pleased;
'*Because I have not known learning*'[1] might be your text."
"Ignorant wretch," said Piers, "you read the bible little;
You study very seldom what Solomon says:[2]
Cast out the scoffer, and contention shall go out with him,
and quarrels and reproaches shall cease."
The priest and Perkyn then disputed with each other,
And their arguing awakened me and I looked all about,
And saw the sun sitting in the south at that time.
Without food or money on Malvern hills,
Musing on these marvels I went about a mile.
Many times these visions have made me reflect,
For the love of Piers Plowman, pensively in heart,
Whether what I saw sleeping might really be so.
But Cato and the canonists conclude against this,
And take this as their text: "Trust not in dreams."[3]
But the bible bears witness to what visions may mean,
When Daniel interpreted the dreams of a king
Who, according to scholars, Nebuchadnezzar was called.
Daniel said, "Sir King, your dream certainly means
That strange knights shall come, to claim your whole kingdom;
Among lowly lords your land shall be divided."
As Daniel had prophesied so it befell:
The king lost his lordship and lesser men had it.[4]
And Joseph dreamed this marvel: the moon and the sun
And eleven bright stars bowed down before him.
"Dear son," said his father, "in famine we shall,
I myself, and my sons, seek you in our need."
It happened as the father said, in Pharoah's time,
That Joseph was a judge who governed in Egypt.[5]

---

[1] Ps. 70:15 (Vulgate). Ps. 71:15 (AV) reads, "for I know not the numbers thereof." The priest's jibe will work only by reference to the Vulgate version of this psalm.

[2] Prov. 22:10.

[3] Distichs of Cato, II, 31.

[4] Dan. 2:39.

[5] Gen. 37:9–10. In lines 142–43 the poet departs from the biblical text, allowing Jacob to prophesy the outcome of the dream, and even to allude obliquely to the death of Rachel (=the moon) in the phrase "I myself, and my sons." In the C

All this compels me to ponder on dreams
Many times at midnight when men should sleep,
On Piers the Plowman, what kind of pardon he had,
And how the priest impugned it, all by pure reason;
And I realized that Do-well surpassed any indulgence,
Biennials, and triennials, and letters of bishops.[1]
Do-well on doomsday will be received with dignity;
He surpasses all the pardons of Saint Peter's church.
Now the pope has the power to pardon when he pleases,
So that people without penance may pass into bliss.
This is part of our belief, as learned men teach us:[2]
And whatsoever thou shalt bind upon earth, it shall be bound
also in heaven.
So I believe loyally, our Lord forbid otherwise,
That pardon and penance and prayers do save
Souls that have sinned seven times deadly.
But to trust in triennials, truly, it seems,
Is less sure for the soul, nor as certain as Do-well.
Therefore I warn you worthies who are wealthy on earth,
If you trust that your treasure will purchase triennials,
Be never the bolder to break the commandments.
I speak mostly to you magistrates, mayors, and judges,
Who have the wealth of this world and are thought to be wise,
When you purchase pardons and the pope's bulls:
At the dread day of doom, when the dead shall arise,
And all come before Christ to present their accounts,
How you lived your life, and observed His law,
What you did day by day, will determine your doom.
Neither a pouchful of pardons nor provincial decrees,
Though you be found in fraternity among the four orders,
And have indulgences doubled, unless Do-well help you,
I would not give for your pardon one paltry pie crust!
Therefore, I counsel all Christians to cry for Christ's mercy,
And to Mary, his mother, to mediate for us,
That God give us grace, before we go hence,
To do such good works while we are here,
That after our death-day Do-well may declare,
At the dread day of doom, that we did as commanded.

---

version, Rachel is kept alive in the interest of symmetry (Skeat, C X 316).

[1] Living a good life (Do-well) surpasses any pardon (indulgence), or masses for the souls of the dead (biennials and triennials) authorized by the church (letters of bishops).

[2] Matt. 16:19.

Here ends the vision of William concerning Piers the Plowman. And now begins the Life of Do-well, Do-better, and Do-best according to wit and reason.

PASSUS IX[1]

Life of Do-well, Do-better, and Do-best

[Prologue]

Thus robed in russet, I roamed about
All summer long, looking for Do-well,
And asked very often of people I met
If anyone knew where Do-well was lodged;
I asked many men who he might be.
No one, as I went, could ever inform me
Where this lad lingered, neither lowly nor rich,
Until, on a Friday, two friars I met,
Masters of the minorites, men of great wit.
I greeted them with courtesy, a decorum I had learned,
And asked them for God's love, before they passed farther,
If they knew any country or neighboring region
Where Do-well now dwelt to direct me to that place.
"Mary," said the minorite, "among us he dwells,
And I hope ever has and shall ever after."
"On the contrary," said I like a clerk, and commenced to dispute:
"Seven times daily, the Book says, the righteous man sins;[2]
And whoever sins," I said, "certainly it seems,
That Do-well and Do-evil may not dwell together;
Ergo he is not always at home among you friars,
But occasionally elsewhere to instruct the people."
"I shall tell you, my son," said the friar then,
"How seven times the steadfast man sins in a day;

---

[1] This section of the poem is entitled *Vita de Do-well, Do-bet, & Do-Best* ("Life of Do-well, Do-better, and Do-best"), and is divided into a Prologue, Passus I and Passus II. To facilitate comparison of this translation with modern editions of the original text, the Passus IX, X, and XI numbering is retained.

[2] Proverbs 24:16, "For a just man shall fall seven times and shall rise again." See Nick Gray, *Modern Philology* 84 (1986): 57–58.

By a parable," said the friar, "plainly I'll show you:
Imagine a man in a boat on a broad bay,
The wind and the water and the wobbling of the boat,
Make the man stumble and fall many times,
For though he stands very straight he stumbles when it shakes.
And yet he is safe and sound and so he should be;
For if he does not rise rapidly and reach for the helm,
The wind would, with the water, overwhelm the boat.
Then were the man lost, through his own negligence.
This is the way," said the friar, "with folk here on earth.
The world is like the water which wanes and waxes,
The goods of this world are like the great waves,
Which as winds and waters wallow about.
The boat like the body is brittle by nature;
And through the fiend and his flesh, and the false world,
The steadfast man sins seven times in a day.
But deadly sin he does not, for Do-well is helper.
That is, Charity the Champion, chief help against sin.
For he strengthens you to stand and steers your soul so well,
That though your body bow as a boat in the water,
Your soul is safe always unless you will otherwise,
Follow your flesh and then the fiend after,
And commit deadly sin and so drown yourself.
God will suffer you to die so, for you yourself have the choice."
    "I have no natural wit," said I, "to know what you mean,
But if I live and look about me, I shall go learn the better.
I commend you to Christ who died on the cross."
And they said the same: "God save you from harm,
And give you grace upon earth to be good to the end."
    Then I went far and wide, searching for Do-well,
And as I went by a wood, walking alone,
The merry songs of the birds made me abide.
And under a linden on a lawn, I lay for a while,
To learn the sweet lays that the lovely birds sang;
The songs of the birds soon brought me to sleep.
Then did I dream the most marvelous dream,
That ever anyone had, from anxiety I think.
    A tall man, it seemed, much like myself,
Appeared and addressed me by my own name.
"Who are you," said I, "who know my right name?"
"One you know well," said he, "and no one better."
"Do I know?" said I. "Who are you then?" "Thought," he replied.
"I have followed you seven years; have you not seen me before?"
"If you are Thought," then said I, "I'm sure you can tell me
Where Do-well now dwells and direct me there."

"Do-well," said he, "and Do-better, and Do-best the third,[1]
Are three fair virtues and are not far to find.
Whoever is meek of his mouth, mild in his speech,
True of his tongue and of his two hands,
And by his labor or his land, earns his own living,
And is trustworthy in his tallying and takes only his own,
And is not drunk nor disdainful, Do-well is with him.
"Do-better does this, but much more he does.
He is as lowly as a lamb, lovely of speech;
Having anything of his own he helps where there is need.
He broke open all the bags and purses
Which Earl Avarice had or any of his heirs;
And with Mammon's money he has made himself friends,[2]
And has entered an order, and interpreted the bible,
And preaches to the people the words of Saint Paul:
'You wise ones, let the unwise live with you for a while,
And with glad will do them good for so God has commanded.'[3]
"Do-best is above both and bears a bishop's crosier
Which is hooked at one end to hold all to good lives.
A spike in that staff strikes down the wicked,
Who watch for any wickedness with which to tempt Do-well.
And as Do-well and Do-better agreed together,
They have crowned one king to keep peace among all,
So that if Do-well and Do-better disobeyed Do-best,
And were rebellious to his bidding and bold to do evil,
Then should the king come and cast them in prison,
And put them there in penance, without pity or grace;
And unless Do-best intercede, abide there forever.
"Thus Do-well and Do-better and Do-best the third,
Crowned one to be king, to work by their counsel,
And govern his kingdom under their guidance;
And not to act otherwise than as these three assent."[4]
Then I thanked Thought that he taught me so well.

---

[1] Here begins the first of several definitions of the triad: Do-well represents the commons, Do-better the clergy, and Do-best the episcopate. Of these three groups depicted in the *Vita* section of the poem, Do-better (clergy) is the most severely criticized.

[2] Luke 16:9. See note to VII, 212 above.

[3] 2 Cor. 11:19, "For you gladly suffer the foolish; whereas yourselves are wise." The foolish attitude that Paul puts on here is used in the poem to hint at the condescension of the clergy toward the people they are supposed to help.

[4] Lines 86–100: This passage describes the relationship of church and state. The bishop teaches the good life, and punishes the wicked, having power over both the commons and the clergy. The king is the bishop's enforcer.

"Yet your speech does not satisfy, so help me God;
I aspire to more knowledge, especially this:
How Do-well, Do-better and Do-best do on earth."
"Unless Wit can direct you," said Thought, "where those three reside,
No one else now alive knows the answer to that."
Thought and I thus for three days we walked,
Disputing of Do-well, one day after another;
Before we knew where we were, we had met Wit.
He was long and quite lean like no other I knew;
No pride in his apparel, nor poverty either;
He was sober in manner and mild in his speech.
I dared suggest no subject to stir up debate,
But I bade Thought to be a mediator between us,
To present a proposition to prove his sharp wit.
Then Thought at that time said these words to him:
"Where Do-well and Do-better and Do-best reside
Will, here, wants to know, if Wit could teach him."

PASSUS X[1]

"Sir Do-well dwells," said Wit, "less than a day's journey,
In a castle made by Nature of four kinds of things:
Of earth and air is it made, mingled together,
With wind and with water wonderfully blended.
Nature has enclosed therein, with consummate craft,
A lady whom he loves no less than himself.
Soul, she is called, coveted much
By a proud knight of France, *Prince of this world*,[2]
Who would win her away with wiles if he could.
But Nature knows his intent and protects her the better,
And has entrusted her to Do-well, duke of these districts.
Do-better, her damsel, is Sir Do-well's daughter,
And serves that lady loyally, early and late.
Thus Do-well and Do-better and Do-best the third,
Are masters of this manor to protect that fair maiden.
But the constable of the castle, who guards them all,

[1] PASSUS X (or Passus I of *Vita*).

[2] Latin *Princeps huius mundi*, from John 12:31, 16:11, etc., referring to the devil, described in the first half-line as "a proud knight of France." By this time (1362) the war with France had been under way for some twenty-five years.

Is a wise knight withal, whose name is Sir Inwit.[1]
He has five fair sons by his first wife:
Sir See-well and Say-well and Hear-well the handsome;
Sir Work-well-with-your-hands, a wiry man of strength,
And Sir Godfrey Go-well, great lords are they all.
These six have been set to preserve the castle;
To care for this woman these wise men are charged,
Till Nature comes or sends to keep her himself."[2]
"What's the name of that castle," said I, "which Nature has made?
And what precisely is Nature; can you please tell me that?"
"Nature," said he, "is creator of all kinds of beasts,
Father and former, the first cause of all,
Who is the great God without a beginning,
Lord of life and of light, of bliss and of pain.
Angels and all things are obedient to His will,
But man is fashioned most like Him in feature and form.
With the word that He uttered animals came forth,
And every thing at His will was wrought with one speech:[3]
For He spoke, and they were made, etc.
Except man whom He made an image of Himself,
Gave him the spirit of His Godhead and granted him bliss,
Life lasting forever and to his lineage after.
The castle that Nature made, *Flesh* it is called,
That is to say, a body with a soul,
Which He wrought with work as well as with word.
Thus through might of His majesty mankind was created:[4]
Let us make man to our image.
"Inwit and all senses reside in that castle,
For love of that lady whose name is Life;
That is Soul, which suffuses every part of the body,
But in the heart is her home, the highest place of all.
She is life and leader and beloved of heaven.
Inwit is the assistance that Soul desires;
After the grace of God, the greatest is Inwit.
Inwit is in the head, and a help to the soul,

---

[1] "Inwyt" is here essentially a synonym for "Conscience."

[2] The soul (a lady since *Anima* is feminine) dwells in a castle (the body), guarded by Conscience and (roughly) the five senses, until in the course of time the body dies and the soul is delivered to God. We might expect Nature (Kynde) to be feminine (Latin *Natura*), but this is not the case here ("himself" in lines 6, 24) or in the following passage (lines 25–41) where Nature is identified with God the Creator.

[3] Ps. 148:5.

[4] Gen. 1:26.

For through his cunning he keeps body and soul
In rule and in reason, unless recklessness prevail.
He urges the eyesight and hearing to good;
Of good speech and cunning he is the beginner.
In man's brain is he active and his power most evident;
There is his bower strongest, unless blood overwhelms him.
For when blood is stronger than brain, then Inwit is bound,
And flesh wanton and wild without any reason.
In infants and imbeciles, Inwit is absent,
And in sots you might see, sitting in the tavern:
They pour ale in their head until Inwit is drowned,
And are brain-mad as beasts, their blood is so strong.
"Then the devil has power, Sir *Prince-of-this-world*,
Over such people; power over souls.
But in children or fools, the fiend has no might
Over deeds that they do, wicked or otherwise.
But the fathers and friends of children are at fault,
Unless they guard them from wantonness while they are young.
And if children are too poor to protect themselves from harm,
Holy Church has the duty to defend and save them
From folly and provide for them until they are wiser.
"But each person in this world who has wise understanding,
Is chief sovereign of himself and must care for his soul,
And keep himself blameless when he becomes an adult.
He must save himself from sin, for so it is proper;
For whether he does well or ill, the wit is his own.
"Then Do-well is a duke who destroys the vices
And preserves the soul, so that sin has no power
To sleep nor to rest nor take root in the heart.
And fear of the Lord is what Do-well uses;
The beginning of goodness is to fear God.
Solomon said it, and it is certainly true:[1]
The fear of the Lord is the beginning of wisdom.
Out of fear, men learn wisdom; Fear is such a master
He makes men become meek and mild in their speech,
And scholars of all kinds to learn well in school.
"Do-better is to be wary of beating with rods.
The psalter says this; you might read it yourself:[2]
Thy rod and thy staff, they have comforted me.
But if Conscience declare that you do well,

[1] Ps. 111:10 (V 110:10).
[2] Ps. 23:4 (V 22:4).

Never in this world should you seek to do better:[1]
    For, *a man is judged by his intention.*
By the counsel of Conscience, in accord with Holy Church,
Direct your mind well and what you do also.
If you act against Conscience you injure yourself;
God's word is witness, and Holy Writ as well:[2]
    He who acts against Conscience, builds up hell.
But if you work by God's word, heed well this warning:
Whatever men say of you, respond not in anger;
Cato counsels this; take heed to his teaching:[3]
    As long as you live uprightly, pay no attention to scandal.
But suffer and sit still and seek no advancement,
And be glad of the grace that God has sent you.
For if you start to climb, and crave to go higher,
You might forfeit your lowliness for foolish pride.
I have learned how unlettered men taught this to their children:
Stones seldom grow mossy where men often tread.
So is it with wanderers who hasten about,
From order to order, always neglectful;
And in those who know many crafts, so learned men say,
Success or prosperity seldom is seen:[4]
    A jack of all trades is master of none.
Paul, the apostle, wrote in his epistle
About some of these people who never stay in one place.
And wisely it is written, and witnessed in churches:[5]
    Let every man abide in the same calling in which he was called.
If you are a married man, a monk or a canon,
Be stable and steadfast and strengthen yourself,
And be blessed for your behavior, yea, beggar though you be!
Complain not to God, though He give you but little;
Be pleased with your portion, poverty or wealth.
    "Thus in fear lies Do-well, and to endure is Do-better,
For through patience you may see how greatness arises.

---

[1] *Intentio iudicat hominem.* A commonplace in canon law. See Alford, *Modern Philology* 81 (1984): 279. This passage (85–113) warns against clerical ambition and greed, like that which was criticised earlier in Passus I, lines 164–73.

[2] *Qui agit contra conscientiam* [*edificat ad iehennam*]. For a similar quotation in the writings of Gratian, Gregory IX, and the preacher John Bromyard, see Alford, *Modern Philology* 72 (1975): 390.

[3] *Distichs of Cato*, III, 3.

[4] Proverbial, e.g., in Ranulph Higden, *Polychronicon*, ed. C. Babington and J. R. Lumby, Rolls Series 41, 9 vols., (London, 1865–86), 2: 170–71. See Alford, *Modern Philology* 81 (1984): 279.

[5] 1 Cor. 7:20.

We learn this from Luke who never has lied:[1]
He that humbleth himself shall be exalted.
From fear and its effects, Do-best will follow,
Which is the flower and the fruit fostered by both.
Just as the rose, which is fragrant and red,
Out of a ragged root and a rough briar,
Springs forth and spreads, so that spicers desire it;
Or as wheat out of weeds waxes from the earth,
So Do-best from Do-better and Do-well may spring
Among men of this world who are meek and kind.
For love of their lowliness our Lord gives them grace,
Such works to work which are pleasing to Him.
"But first and foremost, with folk who are wedded
And live as they promised, God almighty is pleased;
For in wedlock the world stands, whoever will admit it.
They are the wealth of nations, and the root of Do-well;[2]
For from them come those who are called confessors,
Maidens and martyrs, cloistered women and monks;
Kings and knights and all kinds of clerks;
Barons and burgesses and bondmen of towns.
"But false folk who are faithless, thieves and liars,
Were conceived in a cursed time, as Cain was on Eve,
After she and Adam had eaten the apple
Against the order of Him who had made them from nothing.
An angel in anger ordered them out
Into this wretched world to wander and to live
In pain and in labor to their lives' end.
In that cursed constellation they came then together
And brought forth a baby who would bring them much grief.
Cain was he called, in a cursed time conceived;
So says the psalter, you may see it when you please:[3]
He hath conceived sorrow, and brought forth iniquity.
And all who came from Cain's line were cursed by God
And many millions more of men and of women
Who from Seth and his sister soon after were born;
For they married cursed men who were kinsmen of Cain.
Since all who came from Cain's seed were accursed for his sin,

---

[1] Luke 14:11.

[2] Those who marry are a kingdom's greatest asset, and at the same time they are the root of doing well (for "riccheste" read "ricchesse" in 130a). This exaltation of the married state swims against a strong current of contrary opinion. See Morton W. Bloomfield, "Piers Plowman and the Three Grades of Chastity," *Anglia* 76 (1958): 227–53.

[3] Ps. 7:14 (V 7:15).

All who coupled with them, were also condemned.
So God sent word to Seth, and by an angel he said
To keep his kindred from Cain's and command they not marry.
Yet Seth's and his sister's seed were espoused to Cain's;
Against God's command, they begot many children.
Then God was angry, and said to them all:[1]
Penitet me fecisse hominem.
Which is as much to say, in our common speech,
'It repenteth me now, that I have made mankind.'
He came to Noah at once, asked him not to delay,
But swiftly to build a ship with shingles and planks;
Then Noah, his three sons and their wives also
Must hasten to the boat and abide there within it
Until forty days of flood should be fulfilled,
And the cursed brood that Cain made, washed cleanly away.
'Beasts that abound now shall bewail the time
That ever cursed Cain came on this earth;
All shall die for his deeds by downs and hills,
Fish and fowl both, with other fine beasts;
Except for eight souls and two animals of each kind
That in the shingled ship shall surely be saved.
All else shall die, and be condemned to hell.'
Thus through cursed Cain care came upon all,
Because Seth's and his sister's kin were espoused to each other,
Against the law of our Lord lay sinfully together,
And married to their misery, as men still do today.
"For some I see now, and I say what is true,
Out of greed for vain goods against nature are married;
A grievous conception comes from such wedding,
As befell all the people I showed you before.
It is an uncomely coupling, by Christ, so it seems,
To give a young maiden to a feeble old man,
Or to wed an old widow for the sake of her wealth,
Who shall never bear a child, but it be in her arms.
In jealousy joyless and jangling in bed,
Many a pair since the pestilence have pledged them together;
The fruit that they bring forth are many foul words;
No children but chiding and charges between them.
Though they go down to Dunmow (unless the devil helps them)
To seek the side of bacon, they will never succeed.
Unless they both lie, that bacon they lose.[2]

---

[1] Gen. 6:7, translated in line 158.

[2] An ancient custom at Dunmow in Essex of rewarding with a side of bacon any

"Therefore, I counsel all Christians: do not covet to be wed
Out of greed for vain goods or to get wealthy kinsmen.
But bachelors and maidens mate with each other;
Widowers and widows do what is right,
And then you please God, who sends all good things.
But it would be unfit for a man and a woman
To engage in bed-play unless both were pure
In life and in love, and in law as well.
That most secret deed no one should do
With someone who is single, since the law has decreed
That each man have one mate and in marriage be joined,
And do that work on his wife and on no other woman.
Those otherwise begotten are branded as bastards,
False folk and false heirs, foundlings and liars,
Without grace to gain love or any other good,
But wander as wolves and waste what they may.
Against Do-well they do what pleases the devil,
And after their death-day they shall dwell with that wretch,
Unless God will give them grace to amend.
"Then Do-well is to fear and Do-better to suffer,
And so Do-best comes about and brings down pride,
And that is wicked will which corrupts many works."

PASSUS XI[1]

Wit had a wife whose name was Dame Study;
Who was lean in appearance; her expression was sober.
She was obviously angry at Wit having taught me,
And staring at him sternly, Dame Study said:
"Quite wise are you, Wit," said she, "any wisdom to tell
To vagabonds or fools devoid of all sense!"
And she blamed his behavior and bade him refrain
From speaking such words to instruct silly fools.
And then she continued: "Do not cast precious pearls
Before hungry hogs who are happy with haws;
They would slobber on them; slops they'd prefer
To all the precious pearls that in paradise appear.[2]

---

couple who could, after a year of marriage, swear that they had not quarreled during that year.

[1] PASSUS XI (or Passus II of *Vita*).

[2] Paraphrase of Matt. 7:6.

By this I mean simply," said she, "those who show by their works
That they'd rather have land and lordship on earth,
Riches or rents, or rest when they please,
Than all the wise sayings that ever Solomon said.
But now wisdom and wit are not worth a straw
Unless carded with covetousness, as clothiers comb wool.
Those who practice deceit, and plot unjust deeds,
Prevent truth from prevailing by presiding at love-days,
They who master such crafts to council are called
And are treated like royalty who really serve the devil.
Patient Job in his stories spoke of this also:[1]
Why doth the way of the wicked prosper: Why is it well with all of them that transgress, and do wickedly?
But he who has holy scripture ever in his mouth,
And can tell of Tobit, and the twelve apostles,
And preach of the penalty that Pilate imposed
On Jesus the gentle one the Jews drew asunder
On the cross upon Calvary, as the clerks teach us,
Little is he loved for teaching such a lesson,
Or praised or made much of; minstrels know this.
Unless tales of sin assist them (as God is my witness)
More than the harp's music or making of holy verses,
No king nor knight, nor canon of Saint Paul's,
Would give them as New Year's gift the value of a groat.
Minstrelsy and merrymaking among men now means
Lechery and lying and vagabonds' lays,
Gluttony and great oaths are games now-a-days.
"But if clerks and laymen carp about Christ,
At meals, for their amusement, when minstrels are still,
Then they tell of the Trinity, how two slew the third,
And bring forth bald reasons, take Bernard as witness,
And presume in their pride, to prove what is true.
Thus they drivel on their dais to understand the deity,
And gnaw God in their gorge when their guts are full.
But a poor man may cry and call at the gate
Out of hunger and thirst, and trembling with cold;
No one receives him to assist him in need;
He is reviled like a dog and ordered to go hence.
Little does he love the Lord who allows him such blessings,
When he refuses the poor a portion when they need it.
Were not mercy in poor men more than in rich,
Many mendicants might go hungry to bed.

---

[1] Jer. 12:1, but see also Job 21:7.

God is much in the gorge of these great masters,
But among men who are poor are His mercy and His works.
And so says the psalter; seek it in *Memento*:[1]
Behold we have heard of it in Ephrata:
we have found it in the fields of the wood.
Clerks and keen men carp about God,
And have Him much in their mouths, but poor men in their hearts.
Friars and fakers have formulated questions
To please such proud men since the pestilence time;
They defile thus our faith at feasts where they sit.
Every boy is now bold, if he be rich,
To talk about the Trinity, to be treated as a lord,
To formulate fantasies, which injure our faith,
And defame God the Father who fashioned us all,
And criticize the clergy with crabbed words:
'Why would God our saviour allow such a serpent
To beguile the woman, and the man also,
By which desire and deed they went into hell,
And all their seed for that sin suffered the same woe?'
These masters, in pride, propose such vain questions,
And cause folk to falter who reflect on their words.
But Augustine of old against them all preached,
And against all such arguers gave this advice:[2]
Do not seek to know more than is necessary.
Do not wonder why God would ever allow
Satan, the serpent, to deceive His own creatures.
But trust in that tradition which Holy Church teaches,
And pray God for pardon and penance in your life,
And for His great mercy to amend our lives here.
For all who want to know the ways of God almighty,
I would his eye were in his backside, and his heel also.
If any still want to know why God would allow
Satan, the serpent, to deceive His own creatures,
Or Judas, the Jew, Jesus to betray,
All was as He would: Lord, worshipped may you be,
And all shall be as you will, whatever we say!
"And now comes a clod who would pick my brain
How Do-well differs from Do-better! Now let him go deaf!

[1] Ps. 132:6 (V 131:6), which in the Vulgate begins with the word *Memento* ("remember"). God's presence is found in Bethlehem (Mic. 5:2) and in the open country where the poor live.

[2] Skeat cites Augustine's *De Baptismo contra Donatistas*, bk. II, chap. 5. See also Rom. 12:3 (Vulgate) and Alford (1992), 64.

Since he wants to know what they all are:
Unless he live in the least degree that belongs to Do-well,
I dare be his pledge that he'll never Do-better,
Though Do-best drag him along, day after day."
When Wit was aware of what his wife said,
He became so confused he barely could speak,
And as dumb as a door, drew himself to one side.
By no coaxing that I knew, nor kneeling to the ground,
Could I get even a grain of his great wit;
But laughing, he bowed low, and looked up at Study,
As a sign that I should seek her forgiveness.
And when I knew what he wanted, I knelt to his wife,
And said, "Your pardon, Madam, your man shall I be,
To do what you will while my life lasts;
Kindly instruct me in the meaning of Do-well."
"For your meekness, young man," said she, "and for your mild speech,
I'll direct you to my cousin, Clergy is he called.[1]
He has just wed a wife six weeks ago,
Who is sister to the seven arts; Scripture is her name.
These two, as I hope, shall honor my request,
And guide you to Do-well; I dare guarantee this."
Then was I as blissful as birds in the morning,
Merrier than the minstrel who's been given gold,
And asked her the way to where Clergy dwelt:
"And give me some token for him, for it is time that I go."
"Ask for the highway," said she, "from hence to Suffer-
Both-weal-and-woe, if you will learn it,
And ride forth by Riches, but rest not therein;
If you become his companion you'll never come to Clergy.
And avoid the broad lawn that Lechery is called;
Leave it on your left hand a large mile or more,
Till you come to a court, Keep-well-your-tongue
From-lies-and-loose-speech-and-intoxicating-liquor.
Then Sobriety you'll see and Simplicity-of-speech,
Each one of them willing to teach what he knows.
You will come then to Clergy who countless things knows.
Say this as a sign: I set him to school,
And I greet his fair wife, for I wrote her the bible,

[1] The noun Clergy is here used in the sense of "learning," "education." His wife is Scripture because in the medieval curriculum the bible was the central text. In some cases, Scripture can refer to "writing" of any kind, or "books" in general. In the Middle Ages, of course, the literate class consisted mainly of the clergy.

And had her read *Wisdom*, and the glossed psalter.[1]
I taught her both logic and the law also,
And all measures in music I made her learn.
I made Plato, the poet, to ponder his books;
Aristotle and others I taught to argue.
I was the first to formulate a grammar for children,
And beat them with a birch-rod unless they would learn.
For crafts of all kinds, I contrived the tools,
For carpenters and sculptors, and taught first masons,
Showed them level and line, though my eyes are weak.
"But Theology has troubled me ten score times:
For the more I muse on it, the more mysterious it seems;
And the more deeply I explore it, the darker it appears.
It is no science, forsooth, to be subtle about;
Were it not for the love which lies there, little worth would it be.
But since it values love so highly, I love it the more;
For where Love is Lord, grace never is lacking.
Believe loyally in it, if you would Do-well;
For Do-better and Do-best are drawn from Love's school.
In another science it says (I saw it in Cato):[2]
Who pretends with words, but at heart is not a true friend,
You in turn deceive him: thus art deludes art.
But Theology does not teach this, whoever takes heed;
He counsels us the contrary against Cato's words,
And bids us be as brothers and bless our enemies,
And love them that lie to us, and lend to them in need,
And do good against evil; God Himself commands it,
And said it Himself as example for the best:[3]
For it must needs be that scandals come.
"But astronomy is difficult and dangerous to know;
Geometry and geomancy I judge deceptive.
He who studies these three will never thrive,
For sorcery is the chief book employed in these sciences.
Yet are there febicchis of forellis of many men's wits,[4]

---

[1] References are to the apocryphal book of Sapientia (Wisdom), and to the book of Psalms with commentary.

[2] *Distichs of Cato*, I, 26.

[3] Matt. 18:7.

[4] The word "febicchis" occurs nowhere else in Middle English to my knowledge, and therefore remains an enigma; "forellis" can mean "boxes" (OF forel). Most modern editors and translators follow Skeat in his explanation of "febicchis" (Parallel Text Edition, II, 154, note to b.10.211): "perhaps 'contrivances' or 'cheating tricks' suits the context; or it may have been a technical name for some compound substance employed by sorcerers and pretenders to witchcraft." The *Middle*

Experiments of alchemy of Albert's making;[1]
Necromancy and pyromancy, to raise the devil;
If you think to do well, never dabble in these.
These sciences, I admit, I established myself;
Founded them foremost to confound simple folk.
I commend you to Christ," said she, "I can teach you no better."
"Thank you, Madam," I said, and saluted her meekly,
And went quickly away without further ado,
And found as she said, and so I went forth;
Before coming to Clergy I could not stop once.
I greeted the good man as the good wife had taught me,
Then afterward his wife; I was courteous to both,
And whispered the passwords which I had been taught.
No man on earth since God had made heaven,
Was more kindly received nor more graciously welcomed
Than I myself was, as soon as they knew
That I was from Wit's house and with Wit's wife, Dame Study.
Courteously Clergy kissed and embraced me,
And asked me how Wit was and Study, his wife.
And sincerely I said, "They sent me here
To learn from you of Do-well and then of Do-better,
And afterward to see something of Do-best."
"It is an honest life," said he,[2] "among simple people;
Active life it is called; any laborer may live it:
True tillers of the earth, tailors and cobblers,
And craftsmen of all kinds who can earn their own living,
With any true labor, toil for their food,
To dig or to delve, this is called Do-well.
"To break bread with beggars, put clothes on their backs,

English Dictionary (Ann Arbor, Michigan, in progress) reports a suggested derivation from the early alchemist Pebichios: an interesting resemblance, but it sheds little light on possible meanings of the word. Years ago Robert A. Clark suggested to me the possibility that "febicchis" is related to a Welsh noun *bwbach* ("hobgoblin") in which case the reference here could be to a household familiar or spirit like Billy-Blin, referred to in a few of the English and Scottish popular ballads. See David C. Fowler, *A Literary History of the Popular Ballad* (Durham, N.C.: Duke University Press, 1968), 299nn.

[1] Reference is to Albertus Magnus, a prolific scholar of the thirteenth century who was also regarded as an authority on the occult sciences.

[2] Although most manuscripts of the A version have the feminine pronoun, we take the liberty here of reading "he," i.e., "Clergy," who otherwise would have nothing to say to the Dreamer. The distinction between he/she in this poet's dialect (he/heo) could lead to confusion among scribes from other regions; thus it may be that "he" was the archetypal form. Hence we may assign lines 179–215 to Clergy. Scripture then speaks in lines 221–27, 230–49.

Comfort those full of care who in castles are chained,
And seek out the sick and send them what they need,
Obedient as brothers and sisters to each other,
All this is Do-better, as the psalter bears witness:[1]
Behold, how good and how pleasant it is for brethren to dwell together in unity.
'Sigh with the sorrowful, sing with the glad.'[2]
No doubt this is Do-better; Do-best knows the truth.
"Sir Do-best has benefices, so he is most blessed
By what God in the gospel grants us and teaches:[3]
He that shall do and teach, he shall be called great in the kingdom of heaven.
Do-best is, therefore, the peer of a bishop,
Prince over God's people to preach or chastise.
Do-better does well, and is also endowed,
And has possessions and properties for the sake of the poor.
For unfortunate beggars those brothers were endowed,
And that is righteous religion, not running around
Nor leaping over land to absolve wealthy ladies.
"Gregory, the great scholar, a good pope in his time,
Discussed in his *Morals*[4] the rule for religious,
And explained it by example so that each should do better:
'When fishes flee the flood, or the fresh water,
They die from the drought, as they lie on dry land.
So it is with religion: it grows restless and dies,
When out of convent and cloister it covets to live.'
But now Religion is a rider and a runner about,
A leader of love-days and a buyer of land,
Prances on a palfrey from town to town,
A dagger and sword he swings by his side;
God's flesh and His feet and His five wounds,
Are more on his mind than memory of his founders.
This is the life of such lords who should live with Do-better,
And wellaway worse, if I would tell all."
"I thought that kinghood and knighthood and emperors with earls,

---

[1] Ps. 133:1 (V 132:1).

[2] Rom. 12:15, "Rejoice with them that rejoice; weep with them that weep," is paraphrased in this line.

[3] Matt. 5:19.

[4] Gregory's *Morals on the Book of Job* (c. A.D. 590) was one of the most influential biblical commentaries of the Middle Ages. But the text here quoted in lines 204–7 is not from Gregory; instead it is probably one attributed to Pope Eugenius which became a commonplace in the later Middle Ages. Compare Chaucer, *Canterbury Tales*, Prologue A 179–82.

Were Do-well and Do-better and Do-best of all;
I have seen it myself and have since read about it,
How Christ counsels the common folk and teaches this concept:[1]
Princes sit in the chair of Moses.
So I thought that those offices were Do-best of all!"
"I'll not scorn," said Scripture; "unless scriveners lie,
Kinghood and knighthood, for all I can see,
Help not to heaven by one hair's breadth,
Nor riches, nor rents, nor the royalty of lords.
Paul proves it impossible for the rich to have heaven,[2]
But poor men in patience and penance together
Have heritage in heaven, but rich men have not."
"On the contrary," said I, "I contradict that by Christ,
And prove my point by the epistle that Saint Peter wrote:[3]
He that believeth and is baptized, shall be saved."
"In extreme situations," said Scripture, "Saracens and Jews
May be saved in this way; and so we believe
That anyone, in that case, may christen a heathen,
Who for his great faith, when his life fails,
Shall have heritage in heaven as a holy Christian.
But Christians, God knows, come not so to heaven;
For Christians have a calling, a common ideal:[4]
Thou shalt love the Lord thy God . . . and . . . thy neighbor as thyself.
God's word witnesses that we should give of our wealth
To our enemies and to all who are needy and poor:[5]
Therefore, whilst we have time, let us work good to all men, but especially to those who are of the household of the faith.
Creatures of all kinds who to Christ have been likened,
We are charged highly to honor and praise,
Give them from our goods the good we wish for ourselves,

---

[1] Compare Matt. 23:2, "The scribes and the Pharisees have sitten on the chair of Moses." Notice how the Dreamer alters this verse (making "princes" the subject) to support his point in lines 216–17, and perhaps to suggest that high-level government appointees from the ranks of the clergy and episcopate (the equivalent of scribes and pharisees) have turned into regal or princely figures in their own eyes.

[2] See 1 Tim. 6:9, "For they that will become rich, fall into temptation, and into the snare of the devil, and into many unprofitable and hurtful desires, which drown men into destruction and perdition."

[3] The quotation is from Mark 16:16, though the author may also have been thinking of 1 Pet. 3:21.

[4] This line may be modernized more literally as follows: "For Christians have one degree, and that is their common speech." The following quotation is from Matt. 22:37, 39.

[5] Gal. 6:10.

And especially to those who follow our faith.
That is, every Christian should be kind to one another,
And then help the heathen, in hope to convert them.
God never commanded that we harm or kill them,
For He Himself says, in His commandments,
'*Thou shalt not kill*' is the common English:[1]
For, *Vengeance is mine, and I will repay.*
'I shall punish in purgatory or in the pit of hell,
Each man for his misdeeds, unless mercy intervene.'"
Yet I am never the nearer, not for all I have walked,
To knowing what Do-well is deep in my heart.
For whatever I do in this world, whether wrong or right,
I was marked down without mercy and my name entered
In the ledger of life, long before I was born,
Or not written for wickedness, as the gospel bears witness:[2]
No man hath ascended into heaven, but he that descended from heaven.
And I believe in our Lord; no learning is better.
To Solomon, the wise, who wrote the Book of Wisdom
God gave His grace, and great wealth as well,
To govern his kingdom according to his will.
Did he not well and wisely, as Holy Writ teaches,
Both in work and in word in the world of his time?
Who accomplished more than Aristotle and he?
And yet all Holy Church holds that they're in hell!
And there was never in this world two wiser in works,
For all clever clerks, since Christ walked on earth,
Take examples from their sayings in sermons that they give,
And by their works and their words would lead us to Do-well;
And if I work by their works to win a place in heaven,
And for their works and their wisdom wander into hell,
Then I acted unwisely, with all the wisdom that I learned!
On Good Friday, I find, a felon was saved
Who had lived all his life with lying and theft,

[1] The author clearly intended "Thou shalt not kill" (Exod. 20:13), but the text has the Latin for "Thou shalt not commit adultery" (Exod. 20:14). The error could be the author's, or that of an early scribe or rubricator; it is present in nearly all the manuscripts. The additional quotation is from Deut. 32:35 (cf. Rom. 12:19, and Heb. 10:30).

[2] John 3:13. Modern commentators would not interpret this text as supporting predestination. But neither does our author seriously read it thus. The entire concluding passage of the poem (lines 250–303) is in the ironic mode, and consists of a parade of theological absurdities designed to expose to ridicule the "fruits" of book learning.

But by confessing on the cross, and begging Christ for mercy,
He had salvation sooner than Saint John the Baptist,
Or Adam or Isaiah or any of the prophets,
Who had lain with Lucifer many long years;
A robber had remission sooner than all of these;
Without the penance of purgatory, he had paradise forever.
Who might do worse than Mary, the Magdalen?
Or who worse than David, who destroyed Uriah?
Or Paul, the apostle, who had no pity
On Christian people, putting them to death?
And, in truth, there are none holier nor higher in heaven,
Than those who did wickedly, while in this world.
And yet I do not recall, from what five wits have taught me,
That Christ ever commended learning at all.
For He Himself said to some of His disciples:[1]
Dum steteritis ante presides, nolite cogitare.
Which is as much as to say, to men that are unlettered,
"When you are questioned by princes, or priests of the law,
Have no fear at all how you shall answer,
For I shall grant you grace from the God that you serve,
The help of the Holy Ghost to answer them all."
The most esteemed doctor and interpreter of the Trinity,
Augustine of old and highest of the four,
Said this in a sermon (so help me God!):[2]
Ecce ipsi ydioti rapiunt celum, ubi nos sapientes in infernum mergemur.
Which means in our tongue, more or less,
"None are more tempted from the true faith,
Than are these great scholars who study many books,

---

[1] Mark 13:9, 11, "And [when] you shall stand before governors and kings . . . , be not thoughtful beforehand what you shall speak," etc. Note that in the paraphrase of these verses in lines 289–92, an additional set of antagonists is mentioned, "priests of the law" (289), perhaps alluding to Piers' clash with the priest in Passus VIII, 89–126.

[2] St. Augustine, *Confessions*, VIII, 8. The original text reads (in Keble's translation): "The unlearned start up and take heaven by force (cf. Matt. 11:12), and we with our learning and without heart, lo, where we wallow in flesh and blood." Attentive readers will notice that the paraphrase of this in the poem's conclusion (297–303) sharpens the attack on learning and exalts the ignorant poor. But the poet may already have found this form of the quotation in another text. In the *Legenda Aurea*, for example (ed. Th. Groesse, CXXIV, 3rd ed. [1890], 551), we find "surgunt indocti et coelum rapiunt et nos cum doctrinis nostris in infernam demergimur." Notice especially the text in which *indocti* ("unlearned") is replaced by *ydioti*, in Hugh of St. Cher's commentary on Ps. 134:6, as noted by Alford (1992), 70.

Nor are any sooner saved nor more steadfast in conscience,
Than poor people such as plowmen and penniless shepherds.
Cobblers and shoemakers, such ignorant dolts,
Pierce with a prayer the palace of heaven,
Without penance at their parting, pass into high bliss!"[1]

[1] A few manuscripts containing the C-text addition have a Latin quotation following line 303: *Brevis oracio penetrat celum* ("A short prayer pierces heaven"), which is reflected in the imagery of line 302. The ultimate source seems to be Ecclus. 35:21, *Oratio humiliantis se nubes penetrabit* ("The prayer of him that humbleth himself, shall pierce the clouds"). See Alford, *Modern Philology* 72 (1975): 390–91. Three manuscripts contain part or all of an additional passus, apparently written by one John But, who reports at the end that the author, "Wille," has died:

Death dealt him a dint, and drove him to the earth,
And he is closed under clod—Christ have his soul!